ONE WHOLE HEART

MINISTRY

Dedications

This book is dedicated to my three brothers, Mike, Mark, and Paul DeVetter. With the recent passing of my mom, Sharon DeVetter, the dedication, integrity, and family commitment of my brothers was highlighted. Many families focus on the physical stuff with the passing of parents, like the "stuff." My brothers exemplify the desire to place the family relationship as the goal, as well as a commitment to cooperate to protect and nurture my father through the difficulty of the loss of my mother, especially after a decade of being her caretaker and the codependency that goes with that.

I'm thankful to Mark for the constant trips and the work he has done on my father's house as well as purchasing a second house in the town of Tracy to help facilitate time with my parents by the entire family.

I'm thankful for Mike for his constant care, communication, and nurture that he has demonstrated to both my parents.

And I am thankful to Paul for his cooperative spirit that allowed unity in these decisions. I'm also thankful to Paul for his creative and visionary capacity. He goes beyond the societal boxes and releases vision for future and change, not having to look like others. I was extremely honored when he dedicated his second book to me as he began the release process of numbers of books that will be written by the DeVetter family, I believe.

The Second Dedication:

I also dedicate this book to the dedicated One Whole Heart team, which includes all those who considered themselves spiritual children of mine, and the leadership, as well as anyone who has committed themselves as partners with our Lord Jesus Christ to bring healing to the hearts of a vast numbers of people around the United States and in our region without financial gain connected to the One Whole Heart ministry.

This committed team includes those doing One Whole Heart sessions in our area as well as the other locations that have begun to spring up.

It also includes those that are committed to the growth and release of the One Whole Heart process of partnering with the Holy Spirit to heal the hearts as they do the necessary tasks and visions to create an active structure to move further into God's vision to heal the nation.

I also include in this the numbers of people who have participated in the One Whole Heart development in the past eight or ten years and have moved with God to other assignments, some of which have been using the One Whole Heart process tools to bring healing to the hearts in those other assignments.

I do also see the development and release of numerous media resources being released from these I have mentioned, including books, DVDs, CDs, flash drives and movies, to state just a few, to release the revelation that God has inside of each one of these dedicated team members and past team members as well as my spiritual sons and daughters.

Thank you. Again, I say thank you to all of you.

CONTENTS

HEALING THE HEART,
THE INDIVIDUAL AND THE NATIONS

Types of Self-protection

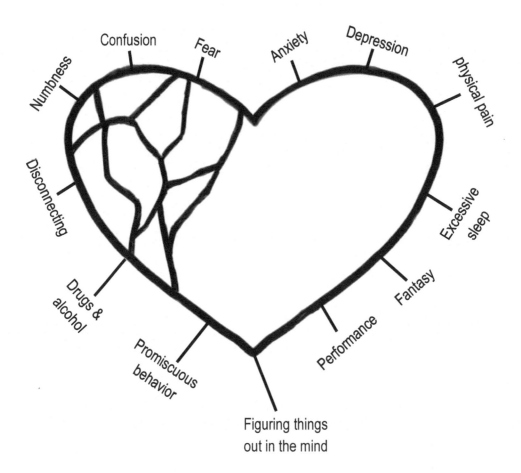

CHAPTER 1

Self-Protection,

the Key to Broken Relationship

What is Self-Protection? Anxiety, fear, anger, sadness, depression, confusion, numbness, disconnecting, figuring things out in the mind, fantasy, excessive sleep or the physical body manifesting pain - these are all types of self-protection.

Every person will do whatever it takes to be protected, including using the methods I have listed above. It might be that instead of depression or sadness or hopelessness, we protect ourselves with performance or drugs or alcohol or adventure or power or various types of sexual activity that is not part of what we were designed for. Anything to give us hope. After all, "hope is the anchor of our soul." That's what the Scripture says. Hope is the anchor of our soul. We have a quest for hope. But these things that we anchor our hope in are temporary. Again, those things that we anchor hope in are temporary. These sources of hope eventually die, one by one. Death of hope leads to mourning, anxiety, sadness, depression, anger, racing thoughts, confusion, disconnection, and isolation. All these are from the flesh, not the physical flesh or body, but our flesh as described in the Scripture. All these feelings represent the flesh dying. We then seek to replace this hope with another hope, perhaps a hope in people, or in places and things; however, that will eventually die also, leading to a deeper root of brokenness or more self-protection.

This is all self-protection and how the cycle of self-protection happens. The only true hope to anchor in is Jesus Christ.

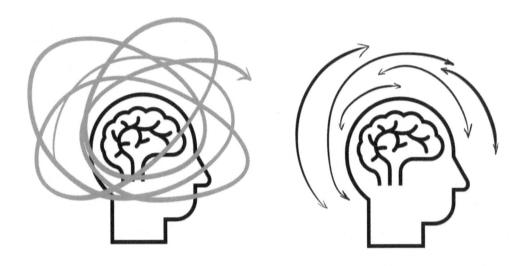

Racing thoughts

CHAPTER 2

Self Protection—Where does it start?

Where does the need for self-protection start? Originally we were created to fully trust and believe God. That changed with the Fall of Adam in the garden of Eden. That opened the door for accusation. Accusation comes out of the fall of Adam. The enemy has right to accuse because of God being a just God. From the fall, all mankind is born in sin. Because of that accusation, we begin to defend ourselves. But this is impossible because we can't defend ourselves. And it's not necessary. But because Satan accuses us (even though he doesn't have the right to because Jesus paid fully for our past, present and future sins), we somehow believe the enemy and his accusations and don't believe Jesus and his shed blood on the cross.

We can't defend ourselves, it's impossible and it is not necessary. We blanket our self-defense with self-protection, such as anger, fear, sadness, confusion and isolation, as well as the other types of protection that I've mentioned, all to defend our perceived loss of value. This actually creates a broken heart that doesn't trust God when the enemy brings accusation or actually starts to blame God as though he is the accuser.

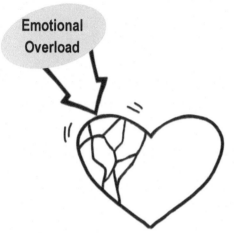

A broken heart occurs because of trauma. Any trauma is an emotional overload that causes our heart to break or sever. I believe out of the components of the broken heart we create anxiety, fear, sadness, depression, many types of anger, and other types of self-protectors.

These are actually perversions of God's original creation. Fear of the Lord and righteous anger are his original creation, not the types of fear and anger that we create to protect ourselves.

These types of perversions actually keep God out or disconnect our relationship with him. Self-protection is the main focus. We use self-protection as though we are the protector, not God. At the time of our original creation, God was our Protector and Provider. God is our Protector. This self-protection is a way of not trusting God to take care of us, but instead that we would protect ourselves, that we are our own protectors.

All self-protection is dysfunctional and not part of our original creation. Self protection happens when the broken heart tries to protect us in anyway separate from trusting God and believes lies about God and ourselves. The broken part of the heart doesn't invite God to protect. God won't force himself or take away our free will. He won't force our choices. He wants in. He's there waiting. He's always been there. He's always been desperately waiting to come into our whole heart. Even the broken part. But the broken part of our heart self-protects and doesn't trust him and won't let him in.

This is the part of the heart that we call flesh, or at least it is connected to the flesh. And not only does it have feelings connected, like sadness and anger, depression and anxiety, it also has thoughts that come and coincide with those feelings.

In Christian circles, we often think that those thoughts are the devil speaking. Although they are his words, most of the time they come from our broken heart. The devil isn't a feeling inside of us. And the thoughts normally, I believe, are coming from our broken heart. I believe that he gets things started and initiates things in our broken heart but most of the words or thoughts that we hear in our mind come from our broken heart. *"out of the abundance of the heart the mouth speaks"* (Matthew 12:34).

The devil comes as the angel of light. He gets things started. He can initiate if he has a license. This ground in our heart is under the control of the devil because we're believing his word instead of God's word in the broken part of the heart.

Most of these thoughts are from our heart. We believe lies in the broken part of our heart.

"Out of the abundance of the heart the mouth speaks" Matthew 12:34 NKJV

15

For example, before I knew the Lord, and even much later, I would have thoughts that would rapidly go through my mind. As I would seek to figure out a solution to my problems in my mind, the thoughts would race. I didn't know that my mind, *"my carnal mind,"* according to the Scripture, could not solve the matters of my heart. I didn't know the racing thoughts were from what the Scripture calls the *"carnal mind."*

The *"carnal mind"* is different than the *"mind of my heart."* God created the mind and all its abilities to compute, to store, to process and function, to serve and support our spirit led by God's Spirit. God is meant to lead. The spirit is meant to be in charge, not the mind. The mind was never meant to be in charge or lead. When that happens, we lose our rest and our peace, whether awake or sleeping. We were meant to be led by God and his Spirit 100 percent of the time. This is called walking in the spirit, being led by God.

> *"For as many as are led by the Spirit of God, these are sons of God." Rom 8:14 NKJV*

> *"I say then: Walk in the Spirit, and you shall not fulfill the lust of the flesh." Gal 5:16 NKJV*

It is not possible to be in the Spirit and have racing thoughts at the same time. The broken part of our heart partners not only with the flesh (that is those negative emotions and thoughts we've been talking about) but it also partners with the carnal mind (the part of the mind that wants to lead or be in charge).

> *"Because the carnal mind [is] enmity against God; for it is not subject to the law of God, nor indeed can be." Rom 8:7 NKJV*

"The heart is deceitful above all [things], And desperately wicked; Who can know it?" Jer 17:9 NKJV

"But no man can tame the tongue." Jas 3:8 NKJV

With this partnership we often think and are convinced that the reasoning or directions our mind takes us is the right direction. It has the focus and the process of the mind leading the way and it seems right. Our mind is sometimes figuring out solutions and creating temporary hope to lead us.

Unfortunately, this hope is only temporary because it is not led by the spirit and not anchored in Jesus Christ. Instead, the hope is anchored in some dysfunctional, temporary way to get value, like a nicer home, a better job or some way to get value from those temporal things that are seen.

I would like to share an example of this from my life. Before I knew the Lord, I was selling residential real estate and constantly needed to be selling something, or buying something, or doing some type of a deal to have hope because the value I had from the last deal was temporary and fleeting. The truth is that as I know my true identity in Jesus and know his love — this becomes my hope, my anchor. It takes away the need for my mind to constantly seek out hope, even through the things that I buy or the things that I create or the things that I do. This positions me in trust or faith to know my true identity. I can then walk out in partnership with Jesus by faith by my calling, which has been written on my heart, on my DNA, and determined by God from the beginning of time. What gets in the way of this is my broken heart that tries to self-protect. It does not trust God. As long as my broken heart is dominant and takes charge, I draw circumstances to my life that reflect my broken heart. This includes things that prove out my belief that I do not have value or there's something wrong with me. Then, out of these beliefs, I live a life of self-protection and I'm led by my own understandings. The key in all of this breakthrough is the healing of the broken heart. When my heart gets healed, through the love of God, as it is written

"...the goodness of God leads you to repentance." Rom 2:4 NKJV

This allows the dominant part of my heart to be led by God's Spirit, so I automatically walk out the call of God on my life.

The broken heart could have happened as early as the womb, when my heart went into overload and broke through experiencing some type of trauma. The broken parts of my heart then formed their own protection systems. As long as this part of the heart isn't healed, it will dominate and stay in control. The motivation of our flesh is to live out of self-protection. This protection includes the carnal mind striving and controlling, even to the point of the mind going into overload. This overload creates numbness, headaches, pressure on the head, neck and back aches, and racing thoughts — all of these keep us from connecting to God intimately.

Intimate connection has to happen in the heart and without it, we are forced to survive through self-protection and operate out of both the carnal mind and the broken heart. That self-protection creates disconnection from God's love. Without the revelation of God's love, we have no capacity for ultimate truth, which is God's truth.

Self-protection causes our capacity to be for temporal truth, not eternal truth.

CHAPTER 3

Multi-Personality

In the secular or clinical world, many labels such as "schizophrenia," "bipolar," and "multi-personality" are commonly used, along with many others. These labels often focus on the brokenness and create an identity in the person based on that. Because you are so-called "bipolar," that is who you are. I do not believe this is biblical. I do not see any of these labels in Scripture. Scripture does say Jesus came to heal the broken-hearted and not that he placed a label on people. Jesus came to heal the broken-hearted. I believe we all have broken hearts and Jesus came to bring healing to all of us.

Our hearts first became broken when we went into emotional overload through some type of trauma that may have happened when we were in the womb or happened multiple times as we were growing up. I believe that we were created that God would protect and provide for us, every second of the day, in all things, as we look to him and trust him. When trauma comes, we are meant to look to God for protection.

When Adam fell and allowed sin to open the door of Satan's accusations that we are bad or don't deserve God's protection. These accusations led to a belief that God will not protect and we need to protect ourselves. This dilemma created a separation or an independence that has caused us to look to ourselves and to others for protection instead of God. But He has always been there every second of every day wanting to protect us.

Because of trauma our broken heart looks to ourselves to protect and not to God and trusts ourselves and not God. We become our own protectors and providers. This self-protection happens because God has given us free will or free choice; he will never force our choice. He will not take away our voice or choice. If we trust him, we choose him. If we don't trust him, he is not invited in to the broken part of a believer's heart and he will not force himself in, even in to the broken parts of our heart. God will not violate the very principle that we, as people, violate and that is often the basis of the broken heart, when someone took away the voice or choice by forcing us.

Trauma most often results from forcing a choice and taking another person's voice away. When an adult physically or sexually abuses a child, that child loses their voice or choice. They would never choose to be treated this way had they had a choice. God will not take our voice or choice away. He won't do it. He has given us free will. When we choose to trust him, we open the door to his protection.

I believe that every person has a broken heart. Every- one has experienced trauma in their lives to some degree or another. The heart can continue to break over and over, as trauma continues to show up.

Actually having a broken heart, according to secular labels, would make us all multi-personalities. The broken part of our heart has a voice that shows itself in our thoughts and visions and dreams and negative feelings. The broken part of the heart formed a dysfunctional self-protection system out of the very ingredients of the heart that God originally created. God created fear, fear of the Lord. Out of fear, the broken part of our heart creates anxiety and lots of dysfunctional types of fear. God created anger, righteous anger, but out of anger, our broken part of our heart creates lots of dysfunctional angers, including depression and wrath.

Through these dysfunctional self-protection systems, we create a system in our broken heart to respond and self-protect. They lead our body based on the understanding connected to this brokenness. Through all this dysfunction we form what Scripture calls the "carnal mind." The carnal mind uses the ingredients of what God created the mind with — reason and logic and all other systems of the mind to pervert the actual function of the God-created mind, so it partners with the broken heart. It takes charge or leadership over our body through faulty reasoning and understanding based on fear, anger, and all the feelings that we associate with the flesh. It's a partnership between our carnal mind and our flesh. They self-protect by trusting ourselves and these dysfunctional protection systems that we created out of our broken heart, instead of trusting God.

This part of our heart we call the "flesh." It operates out of the broken heart that does not know God and does not know God's goodness. Flesh, when dominant in our life, does not trust God and will constantly protect itself. As long as our flesh is dominant, our trust and faith is in ourselves, as well as other people and other things. Because trust or faith is the conduit that invites God in, his invitation to protect is not there. He won't force himself in but waits for that faith and trust invitation.

So if the flesh is dominant, our protection comes from the word that the flesh operates under. We don't believe God's word; we operate under the enemy's word, which is a lie. That's the basis of protecting ourselves. That word says that we are bad, that God will not protect, that God does not love us, that we are dirty, that there's something wrong with us, that we don't have value in the eyes of others or that we just don't have value at all.

Often, someone may disagree and say in their mind "no, I know that's not true," but the broken part of the heart, being independent, believes these lies and shows up and takes charge or dominion. These lies all come from the devil and his word. As a result of believing his lies, he becomes our protector. And obviously he doesn't protect. He came to kill and destroy, as Jesus said in the Scriptures.

God wants to heal the broken-hearted with his goodness. This Goodness includes his truth that's always present in his goodness. As he heals our heart, he heals the root of trauma as it happened, together with eliminating the need for the self-protection system. To heal trauma roots, we ask permission from these broken areas of the heart, first from the self-protection system and then from the root or the initial place of brokenness where trauma first took place. This takes place during a whole-heart process. Getting permission from the broken parts of our heart is important so that God can have an invitation to bring his goodness and healing to the broken parts of the heart.

The self-protection system brings thoughts to our mind and the remainder of our broken heart. Getting permission from the self-protection system allows God to enter these areas that haven't trusted him and he surely comes. He has been waiting and seeking permission to heal every second of our life. He wants to bring healing. He wants to protect. As healing comes, trust comes. Our heart is more and more able to stay in the spirit and operate out of the spirit side, the part of our heart that isn't broken.

What I mean by the "spirit side" is reflective of Scripture: "Those that walk in the spirit will not obey the desires of the flesh," as well as "Those that walk in the spirit are sons of God." The spirit, I believe, is our spirit that is submitted to God's Spirit, the Holy Spirit; the spirit side of us that is led by God. We were created to be totally dependent on God as our Protector and our Provider every moment and not to protect or provide for ourselves. We were created to worship God every second, 24 hours a day, just like the 24 elders and the four living creatures in the Book of Revelation. I believe we are called to replace Lucifer in his vacated position as the angel of worship. We were created to walk in the spirit every second of the day, in that place of worship. What keeps us from that is the flesh, the broken heart, the broken parts of our heart that do not trust God.

It is very important to know when we are in the flesh and when we are in the spirit. Most believers do not understand when they are in the flesh and when they are in the spirit and live a large part of their life in the flesh, which is unbelief. And that is why Jesus calls them double-minded. As long as we do not know the difference, we will live out of the flesh, partnered with the carnal mind. In addition to this, we will attract circumstances to our lives that reflect our flesh and prove our flesh and the beliefs of our broken heart. Beliefs which include "I'm bad and bad things will happen to me," "I don't deserve," "Everything is my fault," among lots of other self-condemning thoughts.

We will talk later about how to recognize when we are in the flesh and when we are in the spirit. The flesh is at war with the spirit (Rom.8:7).

> *"Because the carnal mind is enmity against God; for it is not subject to the law of God, nor indeed can be." Rom. 8:7 NKJV*

> *"The heart is deceitful above all [things], And desperately wicked; Who can know it?" Jer. 17:9 NKJV*

Many of us have been taught to differentiate body, soul and spirit. The soul is the mind, will, and emotions. However, this model does not fully work with Scripture. I prefer to look at it as both our soul and our spirit can be on the spirit side or the flesh side, as well as our body can operate in either the flesh side or the spirit side. This means our body can be led by, or governed by, either the flesh or the spirit.

Take a look at the diagram on the next page to help explain this. As our heart gets healed through God's love, we begin

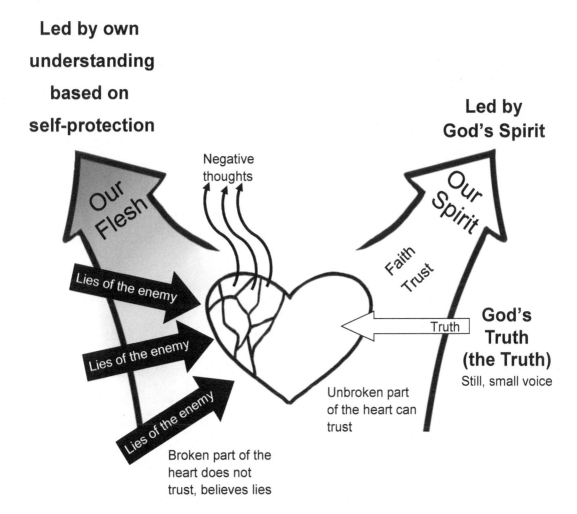

Led by own understanding based on self-protection

Led by God's Spirit

Negative thoughts

Our Flesh

Our Spirit

Faith Trust

Lies of the enemy

Lies of the enemy

Lies of the enemy

Truth

God's Truth (the Truth)
Still, small voice

Unbroken part of the heart can trust

Broken part of the heart does not trust, believes lies

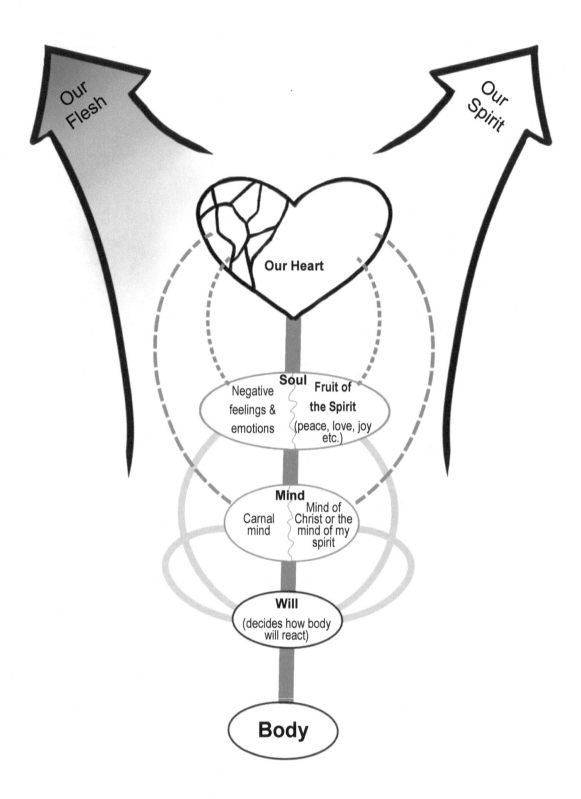

to trust him. This allows us to walk in the spirit more and more, out of our identity, who we really are. We begin to walk in the spirit increasingly more. And through this, our mind and emotions are sanctified. We begin to operate and live out of the revelation of what we were created for, while walking in the spirit more. This revelation is written on our DNA. Scripture calls the mental processing we do in the spirit the "mind of the heart" or the "mind of our spirit," so we have the carnal mind and then we have the "mind of our heart" or the "mind of our spirit" (a different translation converting it to either spirit or heart).

Throughout this book I'm going to refer to the mind of our heart or the mind of our spirit. I'm talking about that place that our mind is submitted to our spirit, which is submitted to God's Spirit and it's not in charge. The carnal mind is that place where our mind needs to be in control, needs to take charge, needs to lead.

This takes place as we walk in the spirit, when our mind, our soul and our body were submitted to our spirit and led by God's Spirit. This walk is how we were created before Adam fell through sin. This walk is the way to live being who we really are, our true self. Again, this is who we really are. Jesus reestablished our ability to walk in our true identity, which is walking in the spirit, through his payment on our behalf of his shed blood on the cross. Through faith and trust in what Jesus did and his love, we will automatically walk out who we are, our true identity, by walking in the spirit. We don't have to self-protect and make things happen.

> [Heb 4:3 ESV] ...*his works were finished from the foundation of the world.*

Through faith, we walk out what Jesus already completed in the spirit. No self-protection, toil, striving, but trust and faith releases forth our call and our purpose.

Crucify the Flesh

CHAPTER 4

How to Know When I'm in the Spirit

As stated in the previous chapter, most believers use their carnal mind and lean on their own understanding to determine or to make decisions. When doing this, even if they try to process through their mental understandings of biblical verses, they are in the flesh. In other words, if I process through my carnal mind even reasoning that is scriptural and place myself under the law of Scripture in order to determine what to do, I'm still processing with my carnal mind and being led by my flesh.

In the spirit, I'm being led by the mind of my heart, that place of God's love, when he is ordering my steps, when I am not trying to keep the law or perform to get his love. I don't need to perform to be loved by God and to get value. I already am loved, and so are you. I already have value, and so do you.

The flesh, partnered with the carnal mind, seeks to work

together to lead our body based on our own understanding, however Scripture tells us:

> *"Trust in the LORD with all your heart, And lean not on your own understanding; In all your ways acknowledge Him, And He shall direct your paths." Prov 3:5-6 NKJV*

Another Scripture speaking of God tells us:

> *"Humble yourselves in the sight of the Lord, and He will lift you up." Jas 4:10 NKJV*

Scripture tells us that:

> *"For the desires of the flesh are against the Spirit…"*
>
> *Gal 5:17 ESV*
>
> *"For though we walk in the flesh, we do not war according to the flesh." 2 Cor. 10:3 NKJV*

The flesh appears as negative emotions, fear, anxiety, worry, anger, sadness, depression, among others, and is that place of self-focus, "my will be done", and self-protection. In the flesh, I am my own protector. When walking in the spirit, I trust God as my Protector. My trust and dependency is on God, not myself or anyone else. Walking in the spirit feels like the fruit of the spirit:

> *But the fruit of the Spirit is love, joy, peace, longsuffering, kindness, goodness, faithfulness, gentleness, self-control. Against such there is no law." Gal 5:22-23 NKJV*

The question in all this is how do I know when I'm in the spirit and when I'm in the flesh? To determine whether I'm in the flesh or the spirit, I can look at which group of feelings I am feeling. The negative feelings that self-protection feels like is what was stated above, including fear, anxiety, worry and anger. All these feelings are aggressive and push and pull us around. They take charge. They need to be in control or in the lead. These negative emotions seek to force decisions by emotionally pushing and pulling us to self-protect. This decision of being forced to self-protect by being pushed or pulled by these negative emotions is walking in the flesh. These emotions try to force us to self-protect. Contrary to this, God will not force our choice. God does not push or pull. He draws us with his love, but he won't push or pull us, or force our decisions or manipulate them. He wants us to freely choose. God created us and gave us free choice. He will never force our choice. People force the choices of each other, which is often the source of trauma. We traumatize each other by taking the voice away of other people. God will never do this. He draws us with his love. Therefore, if I feel pushed or pulled into a decision by the flesh feelings, God will almost always be in the opposite direction of the pushes or the pulls.

> *"For the desires of the flesh are against the Spirit..." Gal 5:17 ESV*

One way to determine whether I'm in the spirit or the flesh is to test my direction as I make a decision using a process called pushes and pulls. The way to do this, also called the heart push and pull test, is to ask the Lord some specific questions. Here's an example of the pull question. I will start by using the first example of me driving down the road. As I'm driving down the road I want to stop and have an ice cream at Orange Leaf ice cream shop. Once, I remember asking the Lord in this situation, "God, if I don't stop and have an ice cream, how am I going to **feel**?" If I feel pulled to stop, as in I can **feel** this strong pull to stop, it indicates my flesh is trying to pull me to have an ice cream. I think all of you can associate with that type of pull. My flesh is saying: **"I want ice cream**." If I do not want to follow my flesh — because this is surely my flesh trying to lead me because of the strength of the pull — my flesh will get stronger if I do have an ice cream and weaker if I go the opposite direction. This is called a pull. My flesh is pulling me to have an ice cream. But if I want to crush my flesh or crucify my flesh, then I do just the opposite: I don't have an ice cream. This does not mean having an ice cream is bad. It only means in this one instance having an ice cream is motivated by the flesh wanting to be in charge. The flesh is at war with the spirit. "I then overcome by the blood of the Lamb."

> *"Then I heard a loud voice saying in heaven, "Now salvation, and strength, and the kingdom of our God, and the power of His Christ have come, for the accuser of our brethren, who accused them before our God day and night, has been cast down. [11] And they overcame him by the blood of the Lamb and by the word of their testimony, and they did not love their lives to the death." Rev 12:10 NKJV*

I can check for pushes and pulls every time. I will now use an example of a push. For example, if you were in a situation that you think God would like to have you take a trip, let's say to Cambodia, but you are not sure whether it is your flesh or the spirit trying to lead you, so you ask this push question: "Father God, if I go to Cambodia, how am I going to **feel**?" Now, you notice in both instances I said, "How am I going to **feel**?" not "What will I think?" It's always a question of "feel".

Let us say you are feeling fear and anxiety and just an overall feeling, saying that I don't want to go, no, no, no. This would indicate that your flesh is not wanting to go. If you don't want your flesh to get stronger, you have to go the opposite direction. By going the opposite direction than where your flesh is leading you, over time you will bring death to the flesh. So by going on the trip to Cambodia, which my flesh does not want to do or is afraid of doing, I crucify my flesh. But I can't do it alone. I have to grab onto Jesus and hold on tight because he's my strength and power to get me from moment to moment and day to day as I walk through the process of going on that trip.

You can't crush your flesh without calling on Jesus for the empowerment. If we try to do it separate from Jesus, it is trying to crush the flesh with the flesh. It does not work. Jesus is at war with our flesh. We give him permission by worshipping and calling on him as we step or go the opposite direction of our flesh, even though the flesh wants to lead. As we step through the flesh, we call on Jesus to empower us: "Jesus, help me." We call on the strength and the power of Jesus as we walk through, weeping and crying before him, "Help me, God, help me."

We go in the direction opposite of the push or pull of the flesh. The flesh is seeking to lead through the negative thoughts and feelings, such as fear, anxiety, anger, confusion, sadness and depression.

Sometimes we have both pushes and pulls happening at the same time. Let's take the last example and ask a pull question: "Father God, if I don't go to Cambodia, how am I going to feel?" Let's say I also feel pulled to go. The flesh is showing up in both directions of this decision. The way I would approach this situation is by asking: "Father God, why is my flesh pulling me to go?" Let's say the answer is, "You will be important if you go." That tells me I should wait to go until the pull to be important goes away. Afterwards I would still go to Cambodia contrary to the feelings of my flesh, those negative feelings that are trying to keep me from going, and grab onto Jesus and crush my flesh.

So this is just my thoughts in this situation and it will vary each time you walk through something like this. The tool that I'm giving you is just a way to look to Jesus for direction. What we are going to talk about throughout this book is various ways to walk in the spirit and to live our lives in the spirit, which is that place of true identity. To do this, our flesh needs to die and needs to be crucified.

"The heart is deceitful above all things..." Jer 17:9 NKJV

"But no man can tame the tongue." Jas 3:8 NKJV

As my flesh dies, God is the empowerment that brings death to my flesh. Not me, not my mind. God is the empowerment. So I can live and walk in the spirit. There is no self-protection in the spirit, only God's protection.

If we walk in the spirit, it is impossible to sin.

"But I say, walk by the Spirit, and you will not gratify the desires of the flesh." Gal 5:16 ESV

"For all who are led by the Spirit of God are sons of God." Rom 8:14 ESV

The spirit is that place of no flesh, total trust in God. All those who have asked Jesus into their heart as their Savior have that place in the spirit where our spirit is submitted to God's Spirit. This is walking in the Spirit, totally obedient to God's will, as my true identity, what I was created for, what is written on my DNA in God's original design. What gets in the way of all of this is the flesh and self-protection, beginning with Adam when Satan first had the right to accuse us because of sin, Adam's sin.

To help determine God's direction and plan to crucify and crush the flesh, this tool may be helpful to you. This is only an example of how to begin identifying the flesh and knowing how to be led by God and walking in the spirit. In further chapters we will go deeper into identifying and crushing the flesh and walking in your true identity.

CHAPTER 5

Protecting Ourselves with

the Ingredients of the Broken Heart

When Adam sinned, the door was open for accusation. Why? Because God is a perfectly just God. Sin brought injustice that needed to be reconciled and paid for. Adam was unable to pay for his sin, as we are unable to pay for our sin.

So Satan, that snake, began to accuse. Satan had the right or the license to accuse because justice was upset and sin was not propitiated or paid for. Through God's plan, he paid the price for Adam's sin and made all things whole. Through the payment of the death of his only begotten son. The just penalty for sin is death. Not only did he repay for that first seed in sin that started it all, he paid for all sin, through faith and trust in what he did, his shed blood on the cross. His love and sacrifice is true. In this way, he not only overcame the first seed of sin, but the roots and the trunk of sin, all sin, by faith and trust in Jesus Christ and that he truly did pay for our sin.

What God established is a means or conduit that would allow all to be redeemed. Trust, which is faith, is that conduit. I think of it this way: blood is the main source of life that interconnects everything in our body: our organs, our tissues, our muscles, everything in our body. If you take the blood out of our body, we surely die. If you take faith or trust in Jesus out of our true connection with God, in the spiritual realm—we die spiritually.

What dying spiritually means is that disconnecting in the spirit from my Creator, from God, and his vision or plan and relationship in my life. Giving myself over to deception and spirits, causing me to self-protect through lust and self-focus and frantically trying to determine truth and my value as a person, separate from God. This determination of truth and value is impossible separate from our Savior, Jesus.

Trying to determine truth being disconnected from God is impossible to do, no matter how many places I anchor my hope. Either I anchor my hope in Jesus or I anchor my hope in people or places or things. Not anchoring in Jesus always leads to how I perform or measure up. Unfortunately, I will sooner or later fall short or not perform well enough and my value will crash as my performance does not measure up. This situation multiplies my need to pay or justify myself where I did not measure up in order to establish my value. Establishing my value on my own is impossible to do. When trying to establish my own value my frantic attempt to get value rests in the hands of people and, worse yet, broken people. As people reject me, or do not listen or hear my voice as my heart seeks value and restoration.

There's no way to accomplish this through these broken people, or even myself. This is because it is impossible for my heart to be restored separate from God, disconnected from Jesus and his shed blood on the cross.

Reacting this way illustrates that I have a broken heart demonstrated by these self protection reactions. Jesus came to heal my broken heart.

> *"He heals the brokenhearted And binds up their wounds." Ps 147:3 NKJV*

> Words of Jesus, *"He has sent Me to heal the brokenhearted." Luk 4:18 NKJV*

As I was growing up, circumstances happened in my life that brought my heart into overload. Because I did not have the ability to trust God as my Protector my heart went into overload. I compensated for this overload by my heart breaking so that the damaged part of my heart will be separated from that which is being protected by the separation. This is a survival process that allows all people to separate the damaged part of our hearts from the part that's not damaged, so that a part of my heart remains undamaged.

The broken heart can continue to break over and over and over from this. The broken part of the heart will always change or pervert out of the ingredients of God's original created heart. We were not created with a self-protection system, which includes anxiety, depression, dysfunctional types of anger, fear, and other self-protection feelings. God did not create these forms of self-protection. God alone is our Protector. I believe we perverted God's original created ingredients of the heart as a means to self-protect through our broken part of our heart. The part of our heart that does not trust God to protect. The broken part of the heart took original created functions (ingredients) like righteous anger given to us as an attribute of our creation and perverted them to dysfunctional angers (wrath) and depression for the purpose of self-protection. Another example is we were created with fear of the Lord. Our broken heart converts this original creation fear into lots of different types of anxiety, worry and panic (among others) all perverted to help self-protect us because our broken heart does not trust God to protect. Yes, you are right, these self protection systems are dysfunctional, painful and plainly do not protect but create further need to be protected.

We make these dysfunctional self-protection systems through the ingredients of our broken heart as we self-protect. We were never created to protect ourselves. Jesus, through his shed blood on the cross, paid the full price for our sins as well as Adam's through faith and trust that his love for us is true and that he actually did pay the price, so I don't have to pay. In this payment, God restored our value. In other words, he has restored my value and your value as a person by what he did, knowing we could not bring healing or restoration on our own.

As I trust what he did is true, I know my value, which was established from the beginning of time, that it is full and complete in him and can't change, no matter what I do or what is done to me. He paid. So I am already restored as I trust in what he did is true.

The part of my heart that isn't broken has the capacity to accept him and believe this fully, but the broken part of my heart doesn't trust God even after I invite him in to the part of my heart that can trust him. This makes me double-minded between the broken part of my heart and the unbroken part of the heart that accepted him and trusts him.

Sanctification is that reconciliation and healing of the broken part of my heart to trust him. In the same way, we have been given the ministry of reconciliation. Reconciling Jesus to the world and Jesus to the church, we also reconcile the part of our heart that trusts God with the broken part of our heart.

God is the one that brings the healing. Anything other than that is just another self-protection system. So as I accept him in my heart, he has my permission in the part of my heart that trusts him to bring his love and continuously show up.

When I'm led by his presence in this, I'm in the spirit. When I'm in the spirit, my spirit, led by his spirit, leads my body. But when the part of my heart that does not trust him takes the lead or control, I'm in the flesh. In this way, there is a struggle between the spirit and the flesh. This makes me double-minded. This is why Paul said in Romans 7,

> *"For I do not do the good I want, but the evil I do not want is what I keep on doing." Rom 7:19 ESV*

This is the flesh warring and trying to be in charge. This leads to self-focus and self-protection. As I crucify the flesh, my spirit takes the lead, guided by the Holy Spirit, God's Spirit, and steers my body. Our spirit, led by God's Spirit, has a still, small voice, just like God's Spirit, the Holy Spirit, not pushing or pulling or forcing its way. In order to hear that still, small voice, we have to be in the spirit. To be in the spirit, we must crucify the

flesh as Paul says,

> *"I protest, brothers, by my pride in you, which I have in Christ Jesus our Lord, I die every day!" 1 Cor 15:31 ESV*

In future chapters, I will talk about the process or practice of crushing or crucifying the flesh. The tongue (a reflection of the flesh) is wicked beyond all things. No man tames the tongue (flesh).

If you are one that has your hope in people and have not taken that first step to invite Jesus to come in and be the Lord and Savior of your life — ask him to forgive all your sins today. Thank him for paying with his life and blood on the cross so that all your sins are forgiven and repent or ask forgiveness for those sins. Ask him, him alone, to come, be your Lord and leader of everything in your life, including your heart, today, and all of the future to eternity.

He will truly come and take residence in that part of your heart that is not broken.

One Whole Heart Process

Healing the broken areas of the heart and inviting Jesus to come with His presence

Sanctification

CHAPTER 6

Crucify Your Flesh

As Christians we seek to walk in the Spirit, God's spirit, the Holy Spirit. This is not about figuring things out in our mind, our carnal mind. It is about trusting God with our heart, our whole heart, as our Savior, our Protector, and our Provider. The flesh can be dominant and through partnership with my carnal mind will lead my body contrary to the will of God. God leads our spirit by his Spirit, which is meant to guide the actions of our body. This is called walking in the spirit or being led by the Holy Spirit. If I am used to being led by my carnal mind or my own understanding and walking in the flesh, how do I change? How do I begin to walk in the spirit?

There are three approaches that will move us to walking in the place of intimacy and connection with God. We were created to live and walk in the spirit 100 percent of the time. This is truly who we are. When we walk in the spirit, it's who we are meant to be. Walking in the flesh often feels and looks like the real thing, but it's actually a deception. Why? Because the truth is, if we spend our time walking out of the flesh, we are not believing who God says we are and we are self-protecting. Our actions are a product of that self-protection and belief. Out of this I perform to try to establish my own value and do things, including sin, to protect myself. I take on these actions as my identity because of my broken heart, believing the word of Satan as he speaks death.

As my broken heart believes the identity that Satan is selling, it partners with these words and takes on an identity of this deception. The broken part of my heart speaks and it repeatedly speaks in to my thoughts. This false identity is lived out in the painful extension of self-protection upon self-protection, upon self-protection, in my flesh. Only intimacy and trust with my Father in heaven can change this cycle. As I invite God into my heart, he will always come. I have the ability to invite him into the part of my heart that trusts, but the part of my heart that is broken does not trust him and does not have the capacity to open itself up to receive a touch of his intimacy that carries the truth of his love. After asking him to take over our heart, we must address the reality that we truly don't fully trust him yet. We aren't fully sanctified. He is waiting to be invited into the remainder of our heart, our whole heart. The One Whole Heart ministry inner heart healing is a very thorough process. It leads to not only getting invitations for God to go into the parts of the heart that are broken, but to witness deep intimacy and to connect the flesh territory in our heart to the spirit territory in our heart, the spirit territory that's connected to God, God's Spirit.

During the One Whole Heart process we also see the carnal mind and its racing thoughts calmed, with numbness and head pressure lifted to allow God's presence to enter these areas of the mind.

To crucify the flesh is to usher God's presence into the broken heart. Through God's love and truth the broken heart converts to spirit and truth and trust in God. Only God can do this. We are there to partner and facilitate his love and healing. God is the only true healer.

Another means of crucifying the flesh is deep intimate worship of God that penetrates our heart. This actually releases chemicals to our brain, such as serotonin and endorphins, that bring physiological healing to the functionality of our brain so it heals the brain/heart. Many functions of the spiritual heart as described in Scripture actually take place in the brain. This is why God has taught us at the One Whole Heart Ministry to do a process called whole-hearting the brain. This invites God's presence into the brain to bring healing chemically and spiritually. God is our Creator and Lord and as we worship him it opens the door for his love to flood our hearts with healing. This healing is not limited to our hearts. Physical body healing is common. The connection of the blood and nerve physically heals in the control center of the brain.

As I previously described, the flesh wants to be in charge and it gets stronger and more dominant as we let it be in charge. When we crucify our flesh and trust God more our flesh, the self-protection dies. The flesh dies. God's at war with the flesh and seeks to bring death to our flesh. Our part in this is to choose to trust God, even if our flesh is violently fighting through flesh feelings and self-protection thoughts to not trust God and self-protect.

When we begin to develop a lifestyle of going the opposite direction of the flesh, it creates death to our flesh and our self-protection. By going the opposite direction the door opens to deeper intimacy, trust, connection and revelation with Father God.

Finally, what greatly aids this process is learning the language of the Holy Spirit. We are spirits with a body. God is a Spirit. God wants us to learn his language. Why? Because as long as we try to communicate with him in the flesh, we will not be able to be led by God.

> *"My sheep hear My voice, and I know them, and they follow Me."*
> *Jn 10:27 NKJV*

When we learn to communicate with God deeper and deeper in the spirit, I believe we can't miss him, his lead, or his direction.

Hebrews 5 talks about drinking milk or eating solid food. The author wants us to eat solid food, become mature. This passage tells us to become a mature son. We need to practice using our spiritual senses, by reason of use, or practice, so we can know good from evil. We cannot know good from evil by leaning on our own understanding, but only by hearing from God in the spirit.

> *For though by this time you ought to be teachers, you need someone to*
> *teach you again the first principles of the oracles of God; and you*
> *have come to need milk and not solid food. ¹³ For everyone who par-*

takes only of milk is unskilled in the word of righteousness, for he is a babe. 14 But solid food belongs to those who are of full age, that is, those who by reason of use have their senses exercised to discern both good and evil.

Hebrews 5:12-13 ESV

What I did in response to this verse was to consistently go to the shelter in Omaha, as well as other similar places. There I prayed hundreds and hundreds of times for people and practiced using my spiritual senses.

The natural man has to go away and we need to learn our true identity, the true paradigm, the spirit realm and the things of the spirit. That's who we really are and that's what should be natural. By practicing, we begin to learn the language of God. By crucifying our flesh, we step into our true identity, our true purpose and calling of our lives, along with the revelations that God has created us with.

This maturity will automatically surface as we crucify the flesh, because it releases trust in our Father and Lord, the Father of Light, the Lord of Lords, the Creator of the Universe, the King of Kings, our Father, Son, and Holy Spirit.

I believe each one of us has written on our DNA revelations to change the world and bring forth the kingdom that far exceeds anything we have ever seen. As we trust Jesus these things automatically will come forth.

Those that walk in the spirit are the sons of God. No one can stop them. No one can stop the call of God on our lives except for our own hearts. As we trust him, the floodgates will open and through us will pour forth God's kingdom. He has already done all these works in the spirit.

> *"...his works were finished from the foundation of the world."* Heb
> *4:3 ESV*

All we do is step towards them, by faith, and pray. They are already in us. They automatically unravel as we trust him. We don't have to make them happen or cause them to happen. They're already part of who we are. As we trust God, his kingdom will automatically come forth through what he already has written on our DNA, the revelations he put in our heart.

CHAPTER 7

Finding That Place of Intimacy With God

As you read in the previous chapter, the fruit of deep intimacy with God is trust. This means less self-protection and less flesh and more intimacy with God. In this chapter, we will focus on two primary areas of intimacy - corporate and individual intimacy.

Corporate intimacy is that place where believers join together and worship God. The more hunger to draw close to know him and trust that he loves us and wants to be close, the deeper the potential connection or intimacy and healing that takes place. Each person will be impacted by God's presence differently. The more our heart trusts individually and the more we hunger and seek his love with an open, tender and sensitive heart, the more impact his presence can have on our ongoing healing. Often, even in the midst of a deep presence of God's love, in the midst of worship, there are people who do not feel or sense God's presence. These people often have an internal thought battle going on in their mind telling them that there is something wrong with them or that God does not love them as much as others or that they don't deserve God's love because of their behavior or sin. Sometimes their thoughts tell them that the other people are foolish or faking the presence of God. What is happening with these thoughts is a result of self-protection from a broken heart. Self-protection uses things like numbness, disconnection, and locking the heart to protect and not letting love come in because somehow love is associated with the pain and trauma from their life. That is part of the brokenness in the heart. This does not mean those that are feeling God's presence don't have areas of brokenness in their heart. Everyone has some brokenness in their heart.

We are speaking about the type of self-protection where the believer doesn't feel or feel as much. The self-protection is keeping this person from feeling. When trauma happens, we all shut down and lock our heart. The more impactful or continuous the trauma, the more we use deeper ways to shut down feelings, including disconnecting from the situation, mentally and emotionally. We use fantasy, sleep, and trying to solve and figure out the matters of our heart in our mind. Our mind, our carnal mind, can frantically search out solutions in the mind to try to solve problems or to protect the heart. The mind has no ability to solve the matters of the heart. When the mind tries to do this, it can force the mind to go into overload. It can show up as racing thoughts and headaches. I believe the use of numbness, disconnecting and disengaging are ways the mind tries to protect itself because of overload. So, as we feel numbness, headaches, or disengaging, normally that could mean that our mind and our racing thoughts are going so frantically that we're going into overload. We compensate by protecting ourselves through the headaches, through the numbness, through the disengaging or similar type of protection systems.

The self-protection use of numbness, disconnecting, disengaging to protect the mind because of overload, creates a problem with feeling intimacy or connection with the Lord. We cannot feel his presence. The numbness and disconnection get in the way. We're disconnected from his emotional love because of the racing thoughts, because of the overload. This includes negative feelings and thoughts that are going on in our mind and the numbness and disconnection that is happening (overload).

If your mind is shut down this way, it is difficult to feel the presence of God. When you don't feel God's peace, love or joy, then condemning thoughts come. They come mostly from the broken part of your heart, seeking to protect in a dysfunctional way. They actually create more fear, rejection, hopelessness, among other feelings, of the self-protecting flesh. I believe most of the thoughts come from what I call the "feeling protectors" part of your broken heart, which I will explain in more detail later. However, because your heart is broken, the devil has license to bring the first thoughts to initiate or trigger the thoughts of your broken heart. After all, you are believing lies in the broken part of your heart and not trusting God. These lies are not based on God's word, but are based on the word denying God's love for you and how valuable you are. Those lies open the door to Satan and give ground or license to Satan to speak life into these lies. As he does, it ignites the hopeless thoughts and feelings of our broken heart, with the end result being overload, or numbness and disconnection in the brain.

I will reveal the solution to this after sharing more about individual intimacy.

Individual intimacy is the place of one-on-one, heart-to-heart connection with Father God, Jesus, and the Holy Spirit. Through the shed blood of Jesus Christ and the presence of the Holy Spirit we connect intimately. We are forgiven, pure and clean. This individual intimacy and love with God heals our broken heart so we know his truth of our identity.

The two biggest obstacles to individual intimacy are time and the mind. Time becomes lord of our lives as we serve it in a performance mode in order to get or protect our value. Often, our thoughts start racing as we are trying to pray or connect with God. Racing thoughts get in the way of intimate connection with God. These racing thoughts are results of self-protection, driven by fear of man or people. Our thoughts are working hard to figure out the matters of the heart, trying to get value before people. We believe if we are valued before people, we will be valued and our heart will be okay. We often search in our mind how to be acceptable before people. Sometimes we even have a series of rules or behaviors that if we perform well enough, we can have value. Anything short of this has our mind frantically searching how to regain value. Another way people try to regain value is by blaming or judging others, so to shift fault or blame from usurping our value. Offense towards people will activate the flesh and initiate racing thoughts. Getting offended starts this process of racing thoughts and the negative feelings of the flesh trying to take charge.

A second obstacle to intimacy is caused by this self-protection process using performance as a way to get value. This self protection process is created when I start to perform to get my value, accomplishing rules that I retain in my heart and get value from any type of performance.

Either way, when our carnal mind takes charge of our actions, our focus will not be on relationship and connection with the Father. We can pray, but we are disconnected and do not feel his presence. Our flesh is in the way of this connection. We can talk at God, but have no heart connection. The reason we don't have heart connection is not because God is not seeking to connect to our heart. He certainly is. The connection is shut down because of these racing thoughts. In addition, many people will have such intense racing thoughts that their mind will go into overload, which will trigger numbness, disconnection, and cause heaviness on the head and neck, including pain or headaches.

To connect with Father God, the carnal mind that is in charge due to racing thoughts has to get out of the way. The only one that can empower this mind shift is God. He has taught us a process we call "whole-hearting the mind". During the process, we speak to the mind as if it was separate and get permission from the mind for God to come into the carnal mind and bring his love. When this happens, God's atmosphere of peace takes over the mind. This opens the door for deep intimacy and connection with God. If you feel numbness, headaches, or disconnection from the mind going into overload, then before whole-hearting the mind, we would speak to the numbness, the weightiness, and the headaches to get permission for Father God to bring his love into these areas of self-protection and as the pressure and weightiness of the head and neck aches go away, then we whole-heart the mind so God's peace can enter. We are actually shifting from the place of our broken heart, the flesh and self-protection into, "the spirit." "The spirit" is the place of us being able to intimately heart-connect with God. Connection intimately with God always happens in "the spirit."

Our goal of individual intimacy with God is to deeply connect our heart with God. To do this, he needs to be our sole focus. I am not talking about talking to God while I'm fixing the car or doing a functional task, or reading a book, even the Bible. These actions can lead to some connection and intimacy. They are important as I am walking with God, connected with him every second of the day. These activities are beneficial, but yet they're limited in deep intimacy because our carnal mind gets in the way of our intimacy.

I am very much in favor of connecting with God in everything I do. As Scripture says,

"And whatever you do, do it heartily, as to the Lord and not to men..." Col 3:23 NKJV

To get deep intimately, God wants to marinate me in his presence. If you marinate a steak for several days and then grill it, that is going to be a very good-tasting steak. In the same way, God wants to soak us in his presence and out of that intimacy comes trust, which is faith and confidence in his love. To do this we must break through the time dimension and stop allowing time to be in charge. It means to disappear through time and to let go of time leading us. When time or people are no longer in the way, then we can connect with God intimately and deeply.

When I first came to the Lord, I used the following method to get to that intimate place with the Lord. What I did is place myself in the same mentality that Jacob had when he said to God, "I am not letting go until I get the promise." And so I would not let go, I would keep pressing in as I prayed, until I broke through into that deep intimate presence. However, now through the method of whole-hearting the mind and whole-hearting my body, we've got tools that can help us get there. These methods help people get to that intimate place quicker with less toil totally focused and dependent on Jesus.

I used to spend most mornings with him and even sometimes all day to get into that place of his presence. I wouldn't quit until I was in his presence. That was the promise I was looking for, his love. I did not do this because I was super spiritual, but "to survive." I needed the connection with his heart to get to the next day. Now today I spend a lot of time with him too, but I get into his presence right away by whole-hearting my mind and my body. I share examples of how to whole-heart one's mind and body on the One Whole Heart website, *www.onewholeheartministry.com*.

God is not only our first fruit, but he is all the fruit. He is the author and finisher of our faith. He's the author of the end-game results. When everything came crashing down in my financial life and my heart turned to him and surrendered to his lordship (at least in that part of my heart that trusted him, "the spirit side") I began to seek him intimately. I got up at 5 a.m. day after day to seek him. At that time what I knew to do was to read the Bible. As I read the Bible, I would often fall asleep. I remember that even if I fell asleep, there was still some connection and love being released to me. Eventually I determined that what I needed to survive was his presence and his love. I continued to seek him in other ways, not only reading the Bible, but my focus was more on intimacy and connection. That's what helped me survive in the midst of the debt, disgrace and humiliation that I was walking through at that time. At times, the only thing I would read would be the Bible, but it was the love, connection and intimacy with God's heart that got me from day to day. It's not about earning God's love by performing and spending more and more time with him. We are already fully loved by God. We can't earn any more love or lose any of God's love. It's about overcoming our flesh, our self-protection, and breaking through the time dimension to be marinated in his love. Oh, how he so loves us.

I notice that in my life I now spend a minimum of an hour or two alone with him each day. I also seek to set aside several times a week where I spend three, four or more hours alone with him. This is merely to illustrate how we break through to deeper intimacy from our need to perform and serve time. In other words, this is how we can break through the time dimension and disappear into him intimately. This is what happened with me. It is not about keeping score. Please do not put yourself under a performance standard based on what I have done. I have a busy schedule, with many things I have to do or could do, or should do. I have to let a lot of things fall to the ground and remain a mess or undone to be able to spend three or four hours with him in a day. In that intimacy and in that connection with God and in that place of walking in the spirit, I can do that and just trust that it's his job to put together the pieces and organize it and that I don't have to carry them. It actually doesn't even work for me to carry these things on my shoulders.

I notice that the greatest shifts in my life, the greatest breakthroughs in my life, are connected to that deep intimacy, those places where I just get lost in him and break through the time dimension and spend hours upon hours with him. Those days of three or four hours or more of deep intimate prayer just shift things, they make a difference, they have impact on what God does and how he moves in my life. He doesn't keep track of the time, but the trust that it puts in my heart and the perspective is what make the difference, that connection and experience of God's love.

A common pattern in my prayer, even though there are some variances, is to whole-heart my mind and then the body, intimately disappearing into him until he brings me out. This is often an hour or two. After that I begin to pray in the spirit over my assignments. Praying in the spirit is a partnership with the Holy Spirit and as the Lord brings to my mind what to pray for, I will pray a short prayer according to my understanding and then pray in the spirit. I pray from that harder place in the spirit to the softer place. I can feel the breakthrough as I pray. Then I'll move on to the next thing God brings to my mind.

I find myself praying each day over and over for many of the same things. That is because things can take a number of years before we see the fulfillment and the fruit, and the victory of the prayer. It is important to be persistent like the lady and the judge in Scriptures. (Luke 18:1-8)

Bill Johnson of Bethel Church says persisting in prayer is like pressing against a large rock and persisting until the rock is finally overcome. All of this praying creates a deeper and deeper saturation in God's love, developing deep trust, with the focus on the Lord. It creates that marination that I talked about earlier.

CHAPTER 8

Broken Relationship

The title of this book highlights resolving broken relationships or at least identifying the source. So what does all this have to do with relationships? Let's discover the rest of this root of broken relationships.

The simple answer is: offense. The root is offense. Getting offended at each other and holding, harboring offenses and allowing them to grow and multiply in our hearts raises up a wall of division and brokenness.

Scripture tells us where offense or fighting come from. This verse states:

Where do wars and fights come from among you? Do they not come from your desires for pleasure that war in your members?" Jas 4:1 NKJV

Offense comes from unmet desires. Desires could be as basic as wanting to have your voice heard, or from looking to the other person to perform or accomplish some task or something to satisfy your needs. Does this mean that if I do not have any desires, I won't get offended? There is some truth to this statement; however, most people who stifle their desires feel in their heart that they don't have a voice. This problem is the basic root of a large percentage of trauma that people carry.

Once we decide in our heart that we don't have a voice, we do one of two things. One is we self-protect and seek to get our voice back by talking a lot, trying to aggressively get our voice back. This does not work. It accomplishes the opposite and no one wants to listen to us. We propel people away. Second is we internalize our anger, which includes racing thoughts of anger. Eventually our anger will turn into to depression and hopelessness.

The truth is, the answer does not rest in people or how people treat us. The answer to the offense must first begin with our own heart and our relationship with God. God wants to protect us and provide for us in all things. People can't protect us consistently. People are broken. When we look to broken people to make us whole, this is called codependency and it can't work. Broken can't fix broken. It's impossible. God is our Protector and Provider. Scripture tells us over and over God is our Protector and Provider. Never once does Scripture tell us that he is only partially our protector and provider. He is 100 percent our Protector and Provider. That means we look to him to meet 100 percent of our needs and we take people off the hook, even if they're in the wrong. We look to God to meet all our needs.

We are created, out of that love from God, to pour out unconditional love to people based on who they are, not what they do, just like God does. His love for us is based on who we are, which he has known from the beginning and he proved this love with his shed blood on the cross. This means that if some-one hurts us or offends us, we stop blaming them even if they're wrong and take responsibility fully for our own heart and feelings no matter who is at fault. We forgive, repent and whole-heart ourselves and take 100 percent responsibility for our own heart, no matter who is right or wrong. Out of this decision, I love people based on who they are, not what they are doing or what they do. I speak life even into those who offend me, as I walk in the spirit and not the flesh, just like Jesus did. This does not take away the consequences for people's behavior. We don't enable them, but only love them and speak life into them in the midst of all of this.

I believe when we love people unconditionally, no matter what they do, and speak life into who they are, we help equip them to walk in who they really are instead of the lies that they are believing about their identity and who they think they are. Contrary to this, if I speak into what I see physically, as though it were the truth or the real, I give life to the lie. What I mean is no person was created to sin. People live out of who they believe they are. When we come to the heart, revelation of God's love, out of that fullness we know who we are and that is what we walk out in our life. So the way to stop sinning is to know God's love, not to focus on the sin and try to stop. This is why Scrip-ture says in Galatians God gave us the law to show us that we could not keep the law separate from his love and his grace and his sacrifice on the cross.

His love empowers us to be who we are according to Scripture, a righteous person, which is why in the spirit we can't sin.

"But I say, walk by the Spirit, and you will not gratify the desires of the flesh." Gal 5:16 ESV

We must identify the real. The real is not what we see. The Scripture says those things seen are temporary, but those unseen are eternal.

"While we do not look at the things which are seen, but at the things which are not seen. For the things which are seen are temporary, but the things which are not seen are eternal." 2 Cor. 4:18 NKJV

The truth is what God says, not what we see.

A person hurts others and sins out of self-protection and believing their identity is based on what they have done in the past, which repeats that same behavior over and over again. However, if they in their heart know their true identity, they will act according to this, which makes it impossible to sin. Every person is truly righteous and that's their true identity, based on Jesus' shed blood on the cross. This is the way we need to see each other and to treat each other with unconditional love. In this, there is no broken relationships. In this, we are living out of the truth, not the lie, those things that are often unseen, which are eternal. (2 Cor. 4:18)

CHAPTER 9

The Carnal Mind, the Basis of Growth in
Much of Today's Church

As long as we are a church that leans on our own under-standing, we are led by the carnal mind and we can never have unity in God's church. Why? Because we are walking in the flesh and seeking to appease the "itching" ears (2 Tim. 4:3). We are looking to give mental or carnal hope to the mind. Scripture tells us that hope is the anchor of our soul.

> *"This hope we have as an anchor of the soul, both sure and stead-fast, and which enters the [Presence] behind the veil" Heb 6:19 NKJV*

In the church we seek at times to generate that hope with mental concepts that have no lasting value. We hope that if we read enough of the Bible that we are justified and have value before God. For a moment the mind is justified because I have read enough of the Bible or performed well enough to have value. Unfortunately, each day I need to perform even more than the previous day. If I go to church enough, do enough at church, go to enough conferences, then somehow each one can speak to my carnal mind and my need to have hope, enough to justify me.

The anchor in all of this can remain based on performance to gain value. Then I do not need to have hope in the cross because I have learned another mental concept that helps justify my value based on my performance. That self-justification will eventually cave in because I cannot continue to maintain that performance each day. My hope is not anchored on Jesus, the rock; instead it is based on the need to get value through self-justifying or self-protecting, by carnal knowledge. The Scripture says knowledge puffs up (1 Cor. 8:1). Our hope must be with Jesus Christ and his finished payment on the cross that fully propitiated our value. He paid the full price. He paid for my past, present, and future sins or mistakes and made me whole, pure, and complete. He totally overcame Adam's fall and made us whole by <u>his payment</u>, not my payment. I can't pay. He already paid the full price. I must have faith that what he did is true. I walk in the full benefit of his payment. I'm fully justified and paid for. I cannot understand this or begin to retain it through my carnal mind. I just can't. I can understand only by revelation of his love through my heart. I need to be touched and connected with God's heart with his love to understand.

<u>Love is a feeling</u> and with this feeling comes a mental revelation of his love in the mind of my heart. I believe when Scripture talks about the mind of my heart, it is the part of my mind that is submitted to my spirit and is led by God's Spirit as I walk in the Spirit.

> *"For this [is] the covenant that I will make with the house of Israel after those days, says the LORD: I will put My laws in their mind and write them on their hearts; and I will be their God, and they shall be My people. None of them shall teach his neighbor, and none his brother, saying, 'Know the LORD,' for all shall know Me, from the least of them to the greatest of them." Heb 8:10-11 NKJV*

> *"Now He who searches the hearts knows what the mind of the Spirit [is], because He makes intercession for the saints according to the will of God." Rom 8:27 NKJV*

Scripture talks about the mind of our heart (or spirit, in some translations). I believe all the abilities, functionality, that is in our carnal mind, is present in the mind of our heart also. That means out of the mind of our spirit I can do math, language, reason, computations, and all the functionality and skills, but this mind is totally submitted to my spirit, which is totally submitted to God's Spirit, as I walk in the Spirit. This is completely different than my carnal mind which wants to be in charge or in control. Unfortunately, what we do in the church at times is to build churches that are focused and speak into helping people anchor on the wrong hope. This carnal knowledge gives tingling ears hope temporarily but does not anchor them in the one and only hope, the Lord Jesus Christ.

As I focus on my physical dream, my dream becomes my

hope. We are in a society today that tells people to pursue their dreams, their hopes, and the church often comes alongside this. Many by the thousands receive these hopes with tingling ears and get on the hope "bandwagon." We are sold and offered this humanistic ideology by secular writers and sometimes even Christian pastors. The truth is our hope can be sinking sand. If it is not on the rock, Jesus, the hope is in the things of this world. Those things that are temporal or seen can eventually lead to destruction. The truth is, God does have dreams he places in our hearts that are automatically released in our life as we trust him as our Protector and Provider. But if the dreams themselves become our protector or provider, that will lead to more brokenness and devastation in the heart because our hopes are anchored in people and performance and not our Father in heaven. We have dreams that fuel our flesh to protect or self-protect. If we pursue these dreams to be justified or to have value, the end result is more brokenness and destruction. It may create a look of success before people, but in the heart the brokenness multiplies, never to find God's love, peace and rest intimately.

The dreams that we have that God implanted in our heart are meant to be walked and lived out, automatically, as we trust him. They are written in our heart. Most of these are outside of our ability to accomplish. Only by walking moment by moment, step by step with the Father as we pray, and step through our self-protection (flesh), then he brings forth the supernatural provision that only he can. These dreams are so much beyond our ability to perform that he is the one who has the power to orchestrate them as we bring them forth by praying and crucifying our flesh. This creates trust and in this unraveling process God brings forth his kingdom supernaturally. We can't boast because he did all the heavy lifting. God often uses this unraveling process in our lives so that we can walk as who we are as sons, not slaves. Yet his glory shows up in the process so incredibly that we know on our own we are helpless and out of this knowledge we can't boast.

In the next chapter I will address this unraveling process that God uses as we walk as sons, not slaves. God wants to bring us beyond the place of being led by our carnal mind and our own understanding. The revelations built inside of us will spring forth because of connection and intimacy with him. Therefore, as a church, our focus should be on that love relationship with Jesus through the Holy Spirit. We should read the Bible not to perform for God, but out of love for Jesus, desiring to be closer. The hunger to draw closer to our Father propels us. God is the God of Scripture and God is the God of structure. Scripture is a type of structure he has given us to bring forth his kingdom by his Spirit, not under the law. I do not believe God's plan is to jam more and more Bible into the carnal mind to meet some performance standard or to generate hope in this performance. Instead, he wants to bring life to the Scriptures we receive and already carry through the love poured out by the Holy Spirit. He wants to make the Scripture and the word that we already have inside of us living and active. So as we read the Scripture, we are intimately connected to him, and it automatically becomes living and active, instead of a carnal word or a law that we have written in our carnal mind.

> *"For the word of God is living and powerful, and sharper than any two-edged sword, piercing even to the division of soul and spirit, and of joints and marrow, and is a discerner of the thoughts and intents of the heart." Heb 4:12 NKJV*

CHAPTER 10

God's Unraveling Process That Brings Us Into Sonship

God created us to walk step by step in intimate relationship with him as sons, not servants or slaves. He created us for this. As a slave, he could give us an order, or directions, as he sends us off to perform these tasks separate from him. As sons, and as heirs, he actually walks step by step with us as part of the unraveling faith walk he has for us. When we walk separate from God, we seek to get our value from how we do the tasks or assignments or how well we perform. If we do well, we have more value than if we don't do as well, which is set next to some standard that people have established.

This is not God's plan. It is man's. Jesus shed his blood on the cross to destroy this plan of using performance to create value. This plan only leads to comparison, competition for value and ultimately brokenness and broken hearts. Under this system we will eventually fall short and come under the judgment of failure to perform well enough to have full value, or even any value at times. As a result of this plan, we are charged with paying for our mistakes by performing or doing something to pay the price to bring restoration. Unfortunately, we do not have the ability or the capacity to pay what it takes to bring restoration. We will always fall short of being justified under this system.

Scripture says if we obey the entire law and stumble at one point, we are guilty of all.

> *"For whoever shall keep the whole law, and yet stumble in one [point], he is guilty of all." Jas 2:10 NKJV*

What Scripture is telling us is that just one sin is rebellion against God and his perfectly just plan. And we can't pay for our sins. We are guilty of all sins if we stumble at one point. Just once.

At the same time, the answer is Jesus Christ and his shed blood on the cross. Through trust and faith in him, he has already paid for each of us fully. Therefore, instead of us seeking to perform to get our value or create our value in ourselves, we already have full value. We do not need to earn it. He established our full value by paying the full price on the cross for all our sins and our mistakes. No one, not anyone, can change that. Not even ourselves. We are fully paid for. We see this truth fully manifest in our lives as we trust what he did is really true.

What is in the way of us living our lives that way? That what we were created for fully manifesting in our life . What is in the way is our broken heart that does not trust or believe and uses the flesh to self-protect.

As I described previously, when I go the opposite direction of the flesh, my flesh dies and loses its empowerment to pull me out of living in my spirit all the time. God walks out this unraveling process with us. He will speak to us through our thoughts, impressions, and spirit connections in the heart with him. He releases vision and directions for us to walk, often in step-by-step increments.

Many times, as we step towards these plans of God, our flesh does not want to go that direction and feelings of the flesh will arise, like anxiety, fear, confusion, and even the feeling "No, no, I don't want to do this." As I pray and connect to God's heart intimately, and as I step through my flesh, as I hold onto God tightly, I will feel lots of flesh feelings, but I step through by holding onto God. "God help me," I cry out. I am positioning my heart to trust him and not trust myself. It seems crazy, but it is believing his word, that he is my Protector, he is my Provider. It is almost like my flesh is going to the cross with him as it dies. This opens the door, as I pray, to trust him more as my flesh gets out of the way. The flesh dying is a process that takes time.

The fruit of these steps is trust and faith. Faith releases the promises in our lives. That's what Scripture says. I believe this opens the door for God's very promises in our lives, so they begin to happen as we trust him in this unraveling process. I see God show up in extraordinary, supernatural ways as I trust him. This is a pattern that I see God use to build and expand our faith, while crushing our flesh, so that we can walk in the spirit, in our identity and calling more and more, walking step by step.

God often can give us a larger picture of our calling that normally would seem impossible or overwhelming. We have no way to walk it out in our own understanding or ability until we learn to walk step by step with him as he unravels our future and the call in our life while doing the supernatural heavy lifting.

Often people go after their call in their own strength and their own understanding. The problem is the fruit is not lasting, because we do this in our own strength and our own understanding. God wants to walk his plans out with you step by step. I believe out of this unraveling, the flesh dies and the revelations we have embedded in our heart are released. In our hearts we carry extraordinary revelations to bring forth the kingdom. They are revealed when the scales of our eyes fall off (Acts 9:18) through death of our flesh, when we are no longer protecting ourselves but trust Jesus fully.

God's unraveling pattern sometimes looks like this. We pray, step through our flesh, pray, and God does the heavy lifting. This is a pattern that I've noticed in my life. God doesn't have to do things the same way over and over. He's got lots of different ways that he can do things, but he tends to be a God of types and shadows or patterns. God often will give us a vision or direction or overall sense of what he has planned or prepared in our lives to bring forth his kingdom. It is all about bringing forth the kingdom of God.

Often we do not have the ability or the capacity to do these things that God created us for. In our weakness, he is strong (2 Cor. 12:9). As we seek him for the first step and each little step thereafter, he will reveal these small steps and it is our part to exercise our faith and make the steps even if the steps are difficult to do. Our flesh uses negative emotions like fear, anxiety, worry, and sadness to keep us from stepping. As I grab onto God with my heart I say, "I'm going to trust you, God, no matter how this feels." I cry out to him for his love and empowerment to get through the step because I can't do it on my own. I need his strength and empowerment.

As I do this, he strengthens and empowers me to overcome my flesh and my flesh begins to die. Wrapped around these steps, I pray into the direction and the vision God has for me. And eventually, he moves supernaturally and moves mountains to bring forth a portion of his plan in my life and even in our corporate lives.

As I keep stepping, praying and crushing my flesh, he leads me. Every step isn't always crushing my flesh but often it can include those places contrary to the push or pull of my flesh.

An example of this is when I built my house in Council Bluffs, Iowa. I was just coming out of a time when I had great debt. I reflect back thinking it may have been more than a million dollars that I was not able to pay. Much of the debt God supernaturally handled in various ways and my trust and faith was increasing. He told me one day he was going to give me a house on a multi-acre piece of land. I had never lived on land larger than an acre, so I was joyful even though I did not understand fully what his plans were. Believing I was being led by the Holy Spirit, I began to open my heart to begin to search out this piece of land. I think God used the first several land locations I looked at to begin the discovery of what God wanted to do. At the same time as I looked led by his spirit I was releasing faith. As I said earlier, our part in our partnership with God is to trust him and that looks like stepping beyond our own understanding by faith towards God in his Spirit-led direction. Even if I make the little steps, my faith is proportionate. I step by faith toward God's direction in relationship with God and connection with him and grabbing onto him and his empowerment.

Our faith partners with God's power, releasing God's plan and promises to us and the world.

Eventually God led me over to Council Bluffs, Iowa, to look at a 33-acre piece of land. While my wife and I were looking at the land, the Lord told me this is where he wanted us to move so he could release the land. I was not 100 percent clear on whether the land we were looking at was the land he was to give us or if it was another parcel in this area called the Wabash Trail. I did understand he was telling me to move my family to Council Bluffs and prepare for the land. I talked to my wife and my youngest son who was going into ninth grade at the time. Somehow God softened their hearts so that they were willing to make the faith move to Council Bluffs, even though we had no place to move and Council Bluffs may have been an undesirable place to move based on their impressions. My wife in her heart, I felt, wanted to stay in Omaha, where relationships were already established.

We began to look for a place to rent. After many months, we could not find a house that would work for my wife's criteria that was necessary if we were to move. Time was running short to make the move in time for my son to start football practice with the local high school. The Holy Spirit spoke to my heart and gave me a vision to make up some yard signs to put on street corners that I wanted to rent a four-bedroom house. I had never seen that done before. The proof it was uncommon were the responses I received, with approximately ten calls from people wanting to rent from me. They clearly misunderstood the sign.

The 11th call was a house way too small and out of the

school district. Only one call opened up the option for a house to rent. The incredible thing about this was that the house we rented was I think I remember from the12th call. This house was not for rent prior to the Holy Spirit having us place the signs. When the owners of the house saw the sign, they contacted me about renting their house to us while they moved to a small town where they had just inherited a mobile home park. The sign actually initiated their desire or vision to do this.

We moved to Council Bluffs by faith, as God opened the door just in time for my son to start football with his new team. We lived in this house in Council Bluffs while we were praying and waiting for the land and the house God had for us. But as we prayed and waited, I continued to do the faith steps that the Holy Spirit would release to me. One of the steps was to call all the landowners along the Wabash Trail and see if they would sell their land or property. As I was able to determine what property was available, there was one 91-acre parcel that I felt I was to have further contact and even an impression that this may be the parcel God was talking about. The dilemma was we had very little money and I had made a conviction and a vow in my heart to never borrow money. I'm not advocating vows, but that's actually what I did.

I had not borrowed any money for the past eight years at that point of the story. For us to buy land and build a house on cash would truly be a supernatural move of God. I had no financial capacity to make this happen and I was not going to toil and try to make it happen with my own strength.

What I was doing was simply seeking God deeper and deeper, intimately, with prayer and meditation and worship and walking out the steps he had me walk even when my flesh fought the steps.

After we began to communicate with the landowners, the Holy Spirit led us to make several offers, which were means for my flesh to arise because all offers needed to reflect our financial ability. We needed to walk in full integrity. We offered options to purchase as well as splitting the land with the options to purchase 24 acres and the additional 67 acres some years later. I don't believe any of these offers were even responded to.

After approximately two years of offers, on the final offer we made, the seller agreed to lower their price to near the offer price per acre, but I would have to purchase all 91 acres, which we didn't have the money to commit to these terms.

A land developer heard of the lowered price and submitted an offer and was able to purchase the property. I remember telling my wife, "The property sold" and she said, "We are moving back to Omaha."

I remember going before the Lord weeping, "God, I just don't understand. I did everything you wanted me to do. I just do not understand." Within 60 days of that prayer, not only had we bought a piece of land, 27 acres, but we were beginning to build the house.

The amazing thing was, as far as I know, the owners of this land did not have the land for sale before the other parcel had fallen through. The piece of land that we bought was very near the one that we were bidding on that was purchased by the developer. The reason this land wasn't available was the County was going to put new electrical grids in and that was one of the two potential pieces of land that they had identified and had some type of an agreement with the owner. And the owner felt that they could not sell the land. But at the time that the 91-acre parcel of land was purchased by the developer, the County had determined that they were going to actually use the other parcel of land in a different area and so this land was now available.

We purchased this land for just a few thousand dollars less than the money we had been able to put in the bank, cash. The Lord was clear that my wife was to pick the floor plan for our house. She picked a small two-story plan but before we could move forward with the plan we had purchased to build, my wife was sure this was not the plan we should build. One day, prompted by the Lord, we ended up in Papillion, Nebraska, in front of a house that duplicated the spiral entry that was in the house we had to sell in the midst of the financial plunge. This house had the floor plan that fit what she had envisioned, but yet did not have the aspects of the house that we had lived in and had to sell that didn't work for her. It was an extraordinary house that would be difficult and expensive to build on the land, along with sewers and septic and a 1200-foot road. We believed God for what he said and with little money in the bank we began to build. What complicated matters more is that I felt like the Lord wanted us to build an ICF house, an all-concrete exterior house with foam blocks of insulation. This type of building system was not very developed at the time in our area when we started building. There were very few tradesmen that had any concept of how to build this type of a home and most homes built this way were simple rectangles, one-story style houses with basements. Our house had multiple angles and, counting the basement, was a massive three-story. It took two years to build the house as we let God arrange the timing and the building process.

At times, funds began to pour in while we were building the house all cash. I remember one of the two years I had sent in our end-of-the-year income taxes to the IRS for $180,000. — and I was so happy to write the check. God had a vision that we stepped into and he was showing himself faithful and supernaturally doing what I had no ability to do on my own. My part was seeking him intimately so that my trust would grow and stepping through my flesh, one step at a time as he directed me.

It was very common for me to spend five to six hours a day with him. I spent this amount of time with him not to perform or earn anything from God. I just needed to connect to his heart to survive and get to that next day.

I still need that deep connection, and I always will even though I spend a bit less time today in direct prayer one-on-one with Papa, (with God). Almost daily in those days of building the house, and even before we had the land, I would battle attacks from people, circumstances, and my flesh telling me this will never happen and condemning me for my belief that God would fulfill his promises. Many, many tears were shed as I held onto the promise that he would finish this good work that he started.

Prior to completion of the house, the money ran out. There was less than 10 percent to be done to complete the house. Christmas and the holidays were coming, so I asked the Lord if it would be okay if I borrowed the money to finish so my family could get in for Christmas. I felt like I was released to borrow some funds to finish but to not encumber the house, to

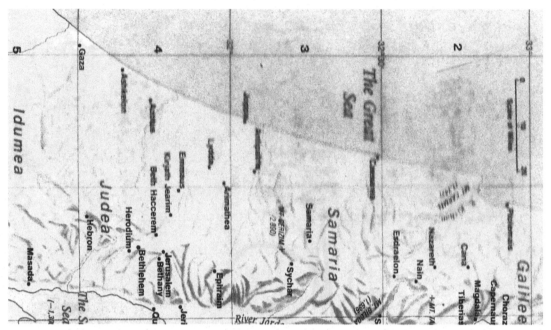

Map of Palestine

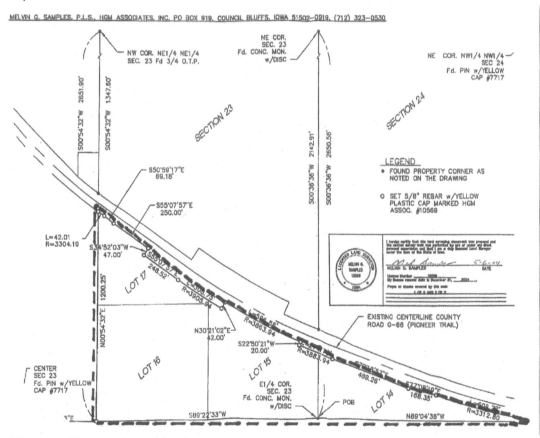

Site plan of the purchased land

leverage the piece of land at the end of the driveway. At this time I had not borrowed any money for ten years, but I decided to take the small loan that a bank offered.

Later, the Lord told me that I could have trusted him for all the money to build the house, but yet I know there was no condemnation that I borrowed the money.

We finished the house and did get moved in. I remember weeping and praising the Lord in all his goodness in this.

After moving in, I decided to sell the end parcel of land that I had encumbered to pay the debt. I didn't feel God would have me live in debt. I made a large sign offering the parcel for sale and began to get a number of calls on the parcel. When this started happening, God brought me into my office in our newly built house and had me take my site plan of the land out and then he had me open my Bible I had at the time to the maps section in the back. And I set them side by side as he had instructed. As I looked, I noticed that the shape of the promised land and the parcels that we had purchased were the same. And as I looked at them, the Lord spoke to me and said, "This is the promised land." Knowing that the promised land is in Israel, I understood he had great plans for this land that he had given us to manage and live on.

Although I had thought all of this was about a house, the house was a small part of what God has planned for this 27 acres land the promised land, in Council Bluffs, Iowa.

After this I did not do anything or step towards anything in regards to the land for several years. One day the Lord spoke to me and asked: "Where is Jerusalem?" I realized he was talking about the promised land. So after a revelation began to go off in the mind of my heart, I confirmed that we had built the house on the very place that Jerusalem is on in the promised land. That is the very highest point in our land and that part of the Promised Land in Israel (similar to Mount Zion on the promised land). That's where we built the house, not knowing that's what was happening.

God began to bring forth further vision of what would go on the land. The artistic rendering on the next page lays the current vision for God and for the promised land as we continue to seek revision and refinement of his plan. Today, the only building on the land is our personal house.

What I did not know until this vision came is that the promised land is one of the ministry centers God will eventually raise up through One Whole Heart Ministry. I see that the unraveling time for the development of the promised land may take place after several other projects, including downtown Council Bluffs and the vision that he has for that area, the Greenwood building and other vision that he's brought forth in his ministry — One Whole Heart in other locations. There are many supernatural things that need to happen to bring the promised land to fulfillment and to bring forth God's vision, including overcoming these present barriers: the 20 to 30 million in funding, the zoning changes, and even bringing my wife's heart in agreement with this plan. All these obstacles seem impossible, but God is beyond impossibilities.

One Whole Heart Ministry

Pottawattamie County, IA

Pottawattamie County GIS
223 S. 6th St
Council Bluffs, IA 51501
(712) 328-4605
gis@pottcounty.com
http://publish.o/
Map Published: 4/26/2015
Map.pottcounty.com

01 CHAPEL
02 MINISTRY BUILDING
03 WORSHIP CENTER
04 PHASE 1 MULTI-USE
05 INDUSTRIAL BUILDING

06 SCHOOL
07 RESIDENTIAL - 28 HOUSES
08 COMMUNITY GARDEN
09 OPEN FIELD
10 TENNIS COURTS

11 304 PARKING STALLS
12 6 PARKING STALLS
13 20 PARKING STALS

Master Plan
4' Contours

BCDM
architects

82

CHAPTER 11

Dying Flesh Versus Death and Mourning

When we have someone close to us in our life that dies, we mourn their loss. Mourning feels like sadness, depression, confusion, anger, fear, anxiety, and many more negative feelings, partnered with negative thoughts that support the feelings. These are the same type of thoughts and feelings we have anytime we are confronting our flesh or when our flesh shows up to take charge.

Mourning is our flesh trying to self-protect in a dysfunctional way. Scripture says hope is the anchor of our soul. We had hope that this person who passed away would be in our life. The hope goes through a death process when the person dies. Mourning is the death of this hope. If you walk through this mourning process in a healthy way, you would seek to anchor your heart in Jesus in the midst of the negative emotions and thoughts. These are flesh emotions as you weep and cry out to God, holding tight to Jesus through talking and communicating and crying out to him. Even if you don't feel him, you will shift your hope from that person being in your life to your hope being in Jesus. Your hope shifts from a person, which is unstable, to Jesus, which is solid as a rock. He is the rock. Your hope in Jesus is solid.

Some people do not mourn and just stuff their feelings, which is also self-protection, and it locks their heart so they don't feel. The result of this is depression, anger, and a locked heart that further self-protects. This will not produce a good result unless healing happens.

The death and re-anchoring process when mourning is the same as any area of our life where we stop self-protecting and grab onto Jesus. We go through the same death and rebirth process as though we were mourning. In this case, we're mourning the loss and being able to self-protect, perform to protect, or get our value from protecting. Instead, we grab onto Jesus and he becomes our Protector instead of ourselves.

Some personal examples of this would be when I stopped trusting myself for money and making money to be secure. My hope in me protecting myself by making money had to die. Me being my own protector had to die. My hope and trust shifted to Jesus being my Protector and my Provider in finances and in life. A mourning process took place as I walked through this.

The same mourning and negative emotions show as the flesh is dying. It is almost like going to the gym. The first day I go and lift weights, I'm not strong. It takes time. It's a process. If I lift the five-pound dumbbells, it will help, but if I lift the plates, the 45-pound plates, my cells will rip and tear more and grow bigger quicker. The same is true as I step through the areas of my own self-protection. God loves me exactly the same whether I lift the five-pound dumbbells or the plates or choose to take the bigger steps or smaller steps to trust him.

An example dealing with the promised land would be that I could have trusted him to make the payments each month and take out the big mortgage and loan on the land and house. God would have loved me just the same. But by taking the bigger step, it was harder and more painful to walk out and took longer to complete than the smaller step, but my trust and faith and intimacy grew bigger and deeper, faster. Death was replaced by life.

This example is true in all areas of self-protection in our life. God is our Protector, not us. When and where are we self-protecting in our life? As we anchor in Jesus we crush our flesh and allow our spirit to lead, led by God's Spirit. God takes his true role in our life as our Protector and Provider.

CHAPTER 12

Ways to Identify the Flesh

The more we know and identify when we are being led by our flesh, which is led by our own understanding, the more we can purpose to move back into the spirit.

Earlier, we talked about catching our thoughts when we are offended or when we are performing to get value. We are going to further develop other ways to identify when we are being led by the flesh. It is important to understand that as we learn to live in the spirit more and more, that place of connecting intimately and being led by the Holy Spirit, we are actually walking in our true self. Who we really are is who we are in the Spirit. That is our true self.

Trusting God to protect instead of self-protecting is what happens when we walk in the spirit. For most of us, this is a new paradigm because we have lived out of what the Scripture calls the natural man all our life, we developed all these self-protection patterns as though this is who we are or as though it is our true identity.

We have been living a lie. The truth is, we are who God says we are: righteous, holy, we are sons and we are heirs to the Throne. Even if I just robbed a bank, this does not change the truth and make me a bank robber. I robbed the bank because I believed the lie about my identity and that somehow I fell short and bank-robbing fit my identity.

If I believe the truth of who I am, that I am righteous and holy, and that this is my true identity, it would be impossible for me to rob that bank. This attack on my identity is a by-product of Adam's fall and Satan's accusations as a result of the fall. We know his accusation is a lie because even if we have sinned, it is fully paid for, as well as Adam's sin, with our Savior's shed blood on the cross. Because of Jesus' payment, Satan's accusations are lies. Whether we sinned even moments before, they are lies. The sins are paid for. If we know his love and his payment in our whole heart, we can't sin.

As I described before, I can't stop sinning by trying harder. I stop sinning by knowing in my heart (not my carnal mind), <u>in my heart</u>, his love and his payment for my sin.

How else do I know I'm in the flesh? Another example of walking in the flesh would be talking or not talking to justify myself. This may be about performance or wanting to be liked or approved by people. If I need to talk or be in control of conversations, events, and people to be okay or comfortable, it may not be the gift of leadership but it may be that this is a way that I stay in control to protect myself.

If you remember the pushes and the pulls, I could ask myself: If I don't talk, how am I going to feel in a particular situation? If I feel pulled to talk, I probably shouldn't. This is different than the Holy Spirit's gentle nudge. This is why we need to learn the language of the Holy Spirit. As we've talked about in previous chapters, often we are fighting to get our voice back. As we fight for approval by talking, some people's motivation is to get their voice back.

With other people, they don't or won't talk and this is their way to get their voice back. Many people seek to get their voice back through internal anger, which turns to depression. Not talking, as well as taking control and talking, are both ways to seek to get my voice back.

The person that doesn't talk and shuts down and uses internal anger or depression actually will find it very difficult to speak in many situations. This is also the flesh keeping them from talking.

To identify their flesh, they can ask God: If I do talk, how am I going to feel? They will feel fear and anxiety or a wall trying to keep them from talking. As long as they let the flesh keep them from talking, they will get more and more angry or depressed and feel they do not have a voice. Their flesh will get stronger or more dominant.

By asking God for his help each time and then beginning to speak, that begins the process of overcoming the flesh for this person.

After all, doesn't Scripture tell us we are overcomers? I believe what we overcome is our flesh. And by this, neither the world nor the devil have a place or a license to be part of our actions. So if we overcome our flesh, we have overcome the world and the devil.

Another area of walking in the flesh is doing things out of fear of people and what they will think rather than fear of the Lord. Fear of the Lord is deep love and desire to connect deeper and more intimate.

Many people do things as a rule, a principle or a law they learned, not realizing that their motivation to follow these principles is actually fear of people. These types of fears create the sheep-like effect that keeps people from being who they were created to be, unique and original. They instead seek to protect themselves by fitting into the box of pleasing people. The walls of the box are their flesh: anxiety, fear, anger, confusion, sadness, depression, etc. The unique call that God has on our life cannot be answered when we fear man and are afraid to stand out, as God releases unique revelations through us.

We are too afraid of man to bring God's kingdom forth. It takes a boldness and an anchoring in God's love to bring forth God's kingdom, not only in word but also in revelatory designs or inventions and expressions he has inside of us. By trusting him, we can walk in all these things without fear of man, no matter what are the perceived consequences.

The term "pride" is often used to cause us to conform. If we don't do what others want us to do, we are being prideful. I see often that humility is a term that coincides with doing what others want us to do, conforming and submitting to man. We certainly need to learn to submit our hearts to authority and each other out of love by the spirit. This is completely different than conforming or submitting under the law. We need to know <u>when we are in the spirit</u> to allow us to be able to be led by the Spirit.

The true definition of pride is "my will be done." That's saying that my personal flesh's will be done. The definition of humility is "thy will be done." God's will be done.

People will often accuse you of being prideful if you don't do the things in the way they want you to do them, especially people that are using control to self-protect. An example of this is when I was on a recent fishing trip to Canada with two of my brothers. Water ended up in our boats from rain throughout the night and the previous days fishing. They thought I should get the water out of the boat the same way that they did, by bailing it out scoop by scoop. This was partly because they had not been on many trips like this before and pulling the plug from the boat while in the water seemed fearful to them. What I did instead is empty my boat by pulling the plug and allowing it to drain out of the back of the boat while going at a higher speed. Then I put the plug back in like I had done numerous times in past years. They may have felt I was being prideful by not doing it in what they thought was a safer way, especially considering that one time the plug popped out while we were fishing and the water started coming in the boat. To them, this verified that I was being prideful. But from my side, I did not need to be afraid because I had done this many times and in my spirit I felt the trust and peace of the Lord. Even when I accidently did not put the plug in all the way one time, I was able to re-plug it and empty it fairly quickly. I was not going to be pulled into their fear in this. They were in a different boat than I was and they were welcome to bail the boat if they wanted. I'm not saying that God would never have me bail my boat. God just wants to lead us step by step each time.

Another example would be when my wonderful wife wants to direct me as I'm driving at times. There are times when her directions are important to get us where we need to go. A couple years ago I was in Minnesota for my mother's funeral and I was driving back to the hotel in a town 20 miles away. I had a route I had decided to take that was fairly simple. My wife, being from Marshall, wanted me to take a different route. It was okay for me not to go the route she wanted me to go. My love for her is the same. She did not lose her voice. She has a voice before the Lord and no one can take her voice.

Sometimes if I listen to people, I am in the flesh because I'm afraid of conflict. Walking while led by God is walking in the Spirit even if it is contrary to what people want me to do, even in little decisions. Other times, if I need to be right to have value (the flesh), that also is self-protection. If I need to be right, arguing the point, that's self-protection. This arguing or frustration is using anger to protect, with the end result of my flesh getting stronger the more I seek to justify myself.

In this case, *"humble yourselves in the sight of the Lord, and He will lift you up." Jas 4:10 NKJV*

In most all these examples, if unsure, you could use the pushes and pulls tool to help determine where your flesh is so you can figure out the direction. We must be led by God, not the flesh nor by people, or our own understanding, and not our carnal mind.

CHAPTER 13

My Trip to Chicago

One day the Lord told me to go to Chicago. I had known there was a Jesus Culture worship conference event going on but I didn't know why he wanted me to go to it. I decided to take the car we gave our daughter to use during college that she had returned back to us. It was a little Rav 4. I thought it would be fun to drive and I would save on gas cost during the trip.

I headed to Chicago. I was able to worship and listen to some Heidi Baker CDs on the way, so it was a wonderful trip. I arrived in Chicago and during the first day of the conference, I got into the car to leave for lunch. I drove by a man that was very large in stature and looking at his face he looked violent. I felt the Lord was saying to me that I was to stop and minister to him. "Oh, really, Lord? Okay."

I pulled the car over and took a hat with me that I had bought at Menard's. I offered it as a gift to him. I ended up praying for him and gave him a ministry card and then went back to the conference.

Towards the end of the meeting that night, I got a call from this man, asking me to come over to his place, which was not far away. I drove over to his place and he asked me to take him to his mom's house, about a half an hour away. On the way he asked me to buy him some cigarettes. I struggled internally but I drove through a drive-through and I bought the cigarettes and we continued to drive out to his mom's house. I was able to pray for both him and his mom at her house. While we were there, he drank a couple of beers. When it was time to leave, he grabbed six or eight beers out of the refrigerator and brought them into my car. They were capped bottles so I did not say anything. We got back into the car, the Rav 4, which was a small car. I was shoulder to shoulder with this very large, violent looking man as we drove. Just a few minutes after leaving his mom's, he lights up a joint of marijuana. I told him he needed to put it out right away. After a short while, he did put the marijuana cigarette out. To me it felt like a struggle to get him to put it out. My flesh rose up after this and I began to have a conversation with God out of my flesh. I asked God, "Why did you have me pick him up? I want him out of my car." I didn't get a response from God until I had got back to the place where I had bought this man's cigarettes. God said to me, as he spoke to me through my thoughts, "You know, there are times when your flesh tries to get my spirit to do things, how does that work out for you?" I answered, also in the thoughts, "It doesn't, Lord. Your Spirit will never follow my flesh. I just do not feel your presence when this happens. My flesh cannot lead your Spirit." The Lord said to me, "You are right. My Spirit will never be led by your flesh, or anyone else's flesh so when you are being led by someone else's flesh, you are walking in the flesh. Anyone else's flesh."

This had a dramatic impact on my life. In the past I would try to figure out what to do in situations by processing it through my carnal mind, according to my own understanding, what was the right and wrong thing to do.

I had a history of doing a lot of ministry to the homeless and the addicted, so I had learned to discern a bunch, but yet many decisions of what to do were processed through my carnal mind. After that day I knew not to lean on my own understanding. If someone's flesh was seeking to lead me, I couldn't follow, no matter who it was -- a leader, minister, or even my wife -- unless the Holy Spirit leads me that direction, not my reason and logic.

An example of this is when this addicted couple would call me and ask me to do things as they sought to manipulate me to help them out of intense jams or difficulties created by their lifestyle. I was immediately able to discern, through the revelation I got on this trip from God, no matter the degree of hardship I was being asked to pull them out of, I needed to be led by God's Spirit and by God, not my own understanding. They were given the option of going through the One Whole Heart process to begin healing of their hearts, which they were unwilling or unable to do. Maybe some day.

God wants to lead us by his Spirit, not our own understanding. It is the only reliable way. Scripture says those that walk in the Spirit will not obey the desires of the flesh (Gal.5:16). In the Spirit it is impossible to sin. We need to learn to walk in the Spirit all of the time.

It is true Jesus wants the whole heart. He is, by the power of the Holy Spirit, seeking to reconcile the entire heart to himself by his shed blood on the cross so that the spirit part of the heart will overcome and dominate, that there would be no provision for the flesh.

CHAPTER 14

Our Relationship With God, How Does It Look?

As I stated in previous chapters, God wants to engulf us in his love, marinate us in his presence, and out of that will come our heart-filled trust of him instead of needing to protect ourselves. What gets in the way of that trust is our flesh and our self-protection. It further locks our heart and causes us to function led by our carnal mind or our own understanding. We are influenced by those flesh feelings that motivate the mind. Those feelings can be fear, anxiety, anger, confusion, numbness, disconnection, fantasy, sleep to protect, and depression, to name a few.

So long as we are led by these and the carnal mind, we will not be able to be led by God's Spirit. The flesh and the mind in this scenario are doing jobs God never created them to do. It is impossible to have unity in the flesh because the carnal mind is unstable. Each person's mental beliefs will be based on their own flesh, guided by their own traumas. In the flesh, our beliefs are often based very highly on our self-developed mental concepts. People will often anchor their trust and hope in these concepts even if more trauma or bad circumstances show up contrary to their mental convictions. Normally they are unable to shift from these convictions because their broken heart and their hope is anchored on those convictions. You find people living under rules and laws or performance heavily in this scenario. There is little ability to fully forgive or release full mercy or grace to others in this. You can find this focus both inside the churches as well as in other life systems, such as Satanism, humanism, or any Christian or non-Christian system that does not fully embrace in the heart the full payment of Christ's shed blood on the cross. Even in some Christian systems we are somehow required by performance to pay part of our redemption. The truth is we can't pay for any of it. And when we know this in our hearts fully, it is not possible for us to walk in the flesh and sin. When we know this fully by God's grace, mercy, and love, we are free. Our spirit already knows this. It's our flesh or our broken heart that doesn't. I believe the broken heart and carnal mind does not only not trust God, but it is capable of all kinds of sin, depending on how extreme the brokenness or the trauma it has endured, even if the person has accepted Jesus. The spirit side of their heart is redeemed with Jesus as Lord of the Spirt part of their heart.

It is true Jesus wants the whole heart. He is, by the power of the Holy Spirit, seeking to reconcile the entire heart to himself by his shed blood on the cross so that the spirit part of the heart will overcome and dominate, that there would be no provision for the flesh.

"But put on the Lord Jesus Christ, and make no provision for the flesh, to fulfill its lusts." Rom 13:14 NKJV

With this understood, you could have a young boy that accepted the Lord and asked Jesus to come take over his heart when he was young. This part of his heart that invited Jesus in is now fully redeemed. Nothing can change this redemption. Yet the part of the heart that is broken can not trust Jesus even though Jesus came into the part of the heart that can trust when that young boy asked Jesus to take over his heart. His broken part of his heart is not redeemed and does not trust God.

This is why Jesus came to heal the broken-hearted.

He heals the brokenhearted And binds up their wounds." Ps 147:3 NKJV

I believe that as this young boy has more and more trauma, this broken part of the heart continues to break over and over and over again. Jesus, through people and circumstances, will be seeking to heal his broken heart. The devil through people and circumstances seeks to multiply the brokenness.

As the heart breaks more and more and partners with the carnal mind and the flesh, the broken heart begins to dominate further, even to the point of acting and leading the body into total unbelief. This young boy, as he grows up, may get into all kinds of sexual perversion, violence, hatred, and even God-hating belief systems out of the carnal mind. I believe that the devil has gone after many of our children and adults that have accepted Jesus. They have a redeemed spirit but the broken part of their heart is inflicted enough with deep trauma that their dominant broken heart takes on an identity to believe they are

Satanists, transvestites, homosexuals, and almost every type of anti-Jesus belief system.

As long as the heart remains broken, to the extent the flesh and the carnal mind accommodate, they will walk as unbelievers and God-haters. As we walk in the healing tools that God is releasing today, we are seeing major breakthroughs of those living under these carnal false identities and their identities are being restored. No one can bring healing to another without the presence and power of God. God is the healer, the only healer. We get to participate in what he is doing. It is the goodness of God that brings repentance. Every day God is releasing more and more revelation of how to partner with him. Ground is being taken constantly. Today people come through One Whole Heart Ministry for anything from 8 to 20 two-hour sessions. The fruit of these sessions is trusting, hearing, and knowing how to step towards the unraveling of God's call in their lives. I believe there will be a time that, collectively, our hearts will be in such a place of trust that his presence will be ushered in so incredibly that the fullness of healing will instantly happen. In seconds people will be healed. Men and women will be healed.

I believe no matter how severely hearts are broken, these hearts will receive God's goodness and healing from the Lord. I believe that we will create a collective atmosphere on earth that ushers in the goodness of God to all men. We will have collective trust as our hearts get more and more healed. It's the goodness of God that brings repentance.

Just as the Gadarene Demoniac became a great evangelist after his encounter with Jesus in the gospel, so will the love of

Jesus and repentance be released to all men on earth through us believers, through trust in Jesus and through his presence being in us. We are to carry his presence and his trust so that the enemy has no place in us and we have no provision for the flesh.

CHAPTER 15

What Do I Do?

As we focus on the healing of the heart through   Jesus, we will be able to trust him more and more. God's kingdom will come forth in our lives. We will no longer want to be clanging gongs and leaning on our own understanding. We will want to walk out exactly who we were created to be, who we <u>really are</u>. That is the person we are when we are walking in the spirit. All men are created to release great revelations for the kingdom to come forth. God has revelations in each of our hearts that far exceeds what the secular world has released and that will fully usher in his kingdom.

In Matthew, the Scripture says:

"And from the days of John the Baptist until now the kingdom of heaven suffers violence, and the violent take it by force." Mat 11:12 NKJV

We need to take the kingdom by force. What does that mean? We need to know what the kingdom is to answer this. Scripture says the kingdom is righteousness, peace and joy in the Holy Spirit. This means that the kingdom is in the Holy Spirit. It also means, looking at the first part of the verse, the kingdom is righteousness, peace and joy.

Let's look at Galatians 5:

"But the fruit of the Spirit is love, joy, peace, longsuffering, kindness, goodness, faithfulness, gentleness, self-control." Gal 5:22-23 NKJV

We see that righteousness, peace and joy fit within the fruit of the Spirit. I believe what this is telling us is to go after the Holy Spirit and the fruit of the Spirit by force, with everything. That means everything.

The next question is, how do we do that? The obvious answer starts by going after intimacy with God, through the Holy Spirit. That truly is the first thing. To do that, we need not only to spend deep, intimate time with the Holy Spirit and crush our flesh as we have been talking about in previous chapters, but we need to learn the language of the Holy Spirit. God wants to communicate with us in the spirit. God is a Spirit and we are spirits with a body. If we communicate with God on the natural or the flesh level, the unbelief and the carnal mind get in the way and we are not sure of who we are or what we should do. Scripture says,

"My sheep hear My voice, and I know them, and they follow Me." Jn 10:27 NKJV

What gets in the way is our carnal mind and the flesh. Neither are part of our original design. We have lived most of our lives as a natural man. That has never been who we are. We need to step into a new paradigm of who we always have been: a spirit man led by God's spirit. That's our true identity.

Hebrews 5 talks about becoming a mature son, eating meat or solid food. It says those that are mature by reason of use have their senses exercised and know good from evil. This tells us we need to practice using our spiritual senses that we may know good from evil.

How do you know good from evil? Not by leaning on your own understanding but by walking in the spirit and knowing the language of God.

As we practice hearing from God, we move from the busyness and the noise of our surroundings to the gentle, still, small voice of his communication. God talks to us through many ways, that is, as we seek him we are in a never-ending process of deepening our understanding. God talks to us through thoughts, impressions, visions, dreams, smells, tastes and feelings, just to name a few ways. As we shift paradigms to the kingdom and the spirit, we are able to understand the communication of God by the Holy Spirit.

I remember, as I began to go to places like the shelter I mentioned in Omaha, I would tell those I was praying for (after getting permission to pray for them) to be patient if I wasn't saying anything. I was listening for the Holy Spirit. I prayed for numbers and numbers of people each week. I would hear or see mostly through my thoughts or imagination or visions and I would take a risk by saying humbly, "I'm seeing this" as I would explain what I was seeing, and ask them if that fits or makes sense to them. My flesh would enter the thought process by coming up with some visions or thoughts to self-protect so I wouldn't be embarrassed by not having a word or a vision to share. The more nervous I would be, the more my flesh would work and try to protect. Out of this practice I learned the difference between visions and thoughts from the flesh and those from the spirit. The more I practiced, the more confidence rose up to know the communication of the Holy Spirit. I began to know more consistently when the Holy Spirit was communicating.

After all, the Scripture says,

"My sheep hear My voice, and I know them, and they follow Me."
Jn 10:27 NKJV

During this time I recall there was a great struggle with my flesh just to go out each day and pray for people. I would be in the car driving to the shelter or wherever I was going and I would have this fight going inside saying "no, no, I don't want to go." My carnal mind would be coming up with good logical reasons why not to go. I would purpose to step through these thoughts and negative feelings and go anyway. After a short time of praying for people, the joy of the Lord would show up.

Most of the time no one would go with me, so I went on my own rather than not go. Because no one was there with me was not an excuse for my flesh to not go. Normally it would have been easier to go with someone. I went to the places I did because I felt this was where God was leading me to go. These places were easier than Walmart or other places, because here most of the people wanted prayer.

Later when I began to teach others to expand their prophetic connection with the Holy Spirit, I would teach them to listen for approximately five different things and either remember them or write them down as they prayed. I told them to listen and ask God questions, such as; "God, tell me something about the heart of this person I am praying for." "God, give me a word of knowledge about this person that I would never, ever know without you telling me." "God, what do you want to say to them today?"

I would teach God's unraveling process in the prophetic release. He unravels to stay in constant communication with us being totally dependent on him. He does this same process as we pray for encouragement, edification, future and hope into people through prophetic prayer. The unraveling process in our daily lives looks a lot like the unraveling process that happens as we're praying prophetically for people. When we begin to speak the five prophetic words, visions or impressions, we mention them one by one while focusing on and <u>listening</u> to our thoughts and visions. We take the risk of speaking these things, as God continues to unravel what he wants to say to the person in each of the five areas as we speak. I teach to take your time and continue to listen while you take the risk of speaking the word or the vision and whatever else you understand as the Holy Spirit releases it. As you listen, God will continue to speak often.

As you begin, you will have a better understanding of some words more than others. Quite often, the ones you have less understanding of that you step out and begin to speak, end up being the most powerful and impactful words.

For example, you may see a vision of a big, fat black cat but do not understand what it means. So as you say, "I see a big black cat," you are listening to the Holy Spirit and he often will tell you more, as the person reveals that they just had their big black cat die and their heart is sad in mourning of the loss. So the revelation for this word was held by the person that you were praying for.

Another good thing about the five topics is that as you begin, if the first one you mention does not click with the person and you are not hearing or seeing anything from God, you can gently say, "that's okay, let's set this one aside and come back to it." And then instead of going off discouraged and the person not edified, you move into the next word that you had written down or remembered of the five topics that the Lord gave you. As you listen, even while you speak, you move deeper into the flow of the Holy Spirit through this process. Always be listening while you speak.

This is a great way to learn. I normally used to like to start with the word about the heart first. I found this would move me into unraveling right away and add to encouragement and build the person up right from the start, even if the word revealed past brokenness. God will wrap all this into a future and a hope in their true identity and it would end up being an encouraging word because prophecy edifies and builds up. It doesn't tear down.

Personally, I do not do the five-topic process anymore myself. At one point after using this to develop my ability to understand and hear, God showed me to start with the very first word and let everything be unraveled at once, in order to further develop the unraveling process in me. In other words, starting only with the first word, not looking for any other words, and letting him unravel the whole thing as I listened and spoke and released prophetic word. This was done, I believe, to further develop and multiply my prophetic process of listening to God and releasing his word, moment by moment, thought by thought and vision by vision.

Our true identity comes forth as we learn the language of the Holy Spirit. As we focus on the healing of our hearts, we can consistently live out of His rest and intimacy with God.

"Therefore, since a promise remains of entering His rest, let us fear lest any of you seem to have come short of it. 2 For indeed the gospel was preached to us as well as to them; but the word which they heard did not profit them, not being mixed with faith in those who heard [it]. 3 For we who have believed do enter that rest, as He has said: 'So I swore in My wrath, 'They shall not enter My rest,' ' although the works were finished from the foundation of the world. 4 For He has spoken in a certain place of the seventh [day] in this way: 'And God rested on the seventh day from all His works' : 5 and again in this [place]: 'They shall not enter My rest.' 6 Since therefore it remains that some [must] enter it, and those to whom it was first preached did not enter because of disobedience, 7 again He designates a certain day, saying in David, 'Today,' after such a long time, as it has been said: 'Today, if you will hear His voice, Do not harden your hearts.' 8 For if Joshua had given them rest, then He would not afterward have spoken of another day. 9 There remains therefore a rest for the people of God. 10 For he who has entered His rest has himself also ceased from his works as God [did] from His. 11 Let us therefore be diligent to enter that rest, lest anyone fall according to the same example of disobedience. 12 For the word of God is living and powerful, and sharper than any two-edged sword, piercing even to the division of soul and spirit, and of joints and marrow, and is

a discerner of the thoughts and intents of the heart. 13 And there is no creature hidden from His sight, but all things are naked and open to the eyes of Him to whom we [must give] account." Heb 4:1-13 NKJV

Our true identity comes forth and we consistently walk in the spirit purposely taking the kingdom by force as a result of stepping through and crushing the flesh. When flesh gets crucified that makes way for living out of Gods rest as the works he already finished from the foundation of the world automatically come forth in our life.

CHAPTER 16

Concepts to Overcome the

Broken Heart and Walk in the Spirit

Embrace Failure, Order, Disorder, Discipline, Self-Control Growing in God and Not Limit Yourself

God of Peace Versus the Flesh

Many people often go to church to listen to preaching and focus on being "all in" after God.

> *"For whoever desires to save his life will lose it, but whoever loses his life for My sake will find it." Mat 16:25 NKJV*

We get excited about being "all in," but we don't know what this looks like. Our flesh will point out how we fall short. We walk around in shame and guilt because we are not performing well enough to be all in. We are always falling short, failing, or sinning even to the point we feel God is mad at us for not measuring up. Mentally, all this comes out of performance to get our value. This need to perform is multiplied through trauma and disconnection with our parents, and later expanded through other people in our lives, as we create this performance lifestyle. As our heart let's go of the old roots and trauma and I get a revelation of God's unconditional love, I no longer need to live in this pattern of feeling like I'm falling short. One of the things that needs to happen for me to accomplish this is for me to crucify my flesh, that is, crucify the old patterns that want to attach to new or current offenses. My flesh does not want to die. My flesh fights desperately to live but I immediately forgive, repent, whole-heart myself of the offense. I get back into the spirit and worship God. These old patterns will go away as I whole-heart myself and the flesh dies (whole – hearting yourself is on the front page of our website, www.onewholeheartministry.com).

There are a couple more concepts that help me identify my flesh and step through my flesh to overcome. The first one I'm going to tell you about is to embrace failure. Failure is a concept the world has created that tells us according to some standard determined by some value system, whether I have value or how much value I have. The truth is my value is not determined by anyone's value system. No matter how good and just this value system is, my value was established from the beginning of time. God knew me from the beginning of time. There is no time dimension in heaven or in the kingdom. When Adam sinned, as we spoke of earlier, Satan began to accuse based on the injustice created by sin. Jesus shed his blood on the cross and canceled all accusation and paid the full price for all our sins, mistakes, or failures. Jesus made it impossible for me to fail. Because of this, my mistakes are fully paid for, past, present and future mistakes. My failures are totally paid for. My value was fully established, paid for, no matter what I have done or what has been done to me. Yes, my value is totally paid for. No one can legally accuse me, no matter what sin or mistake I've done. They are already paid for.

As we spoke of earlier, the revelation of God's love in this is the very thing that keeps me from sinning. Given this truth, even if I do something that does not seem to measure up to someone's standard, it does not make me a failure. The truth is just the opposite. It is impossible for me to fail from a value standpoint. When I know in my heart that it is impossible to fail, I begin to have victory over failure. Failure no longer has sting. Failure no longer has a grip on me.

When Jesus was in the process of moving towards his crucifixion, he did not run and hide from death. He actually stepped in God's will for his crucifixion, his death. He overcame death by being anchored to the Father and not fearing death but instead stepping into death. He overcame death and gave life to all men through our trust in Jesus.

In the same way, as we believe what was done on the cross actually happened and that Jesus overcame death but also overcame failure, we are no longer subject to the fear of failure. If the fear of death has no sting, failure has no sting also. If we fear failure, then it also has sting.

As our heart trusts that Jesus' shed blood on the cross actually happened and we believe the truth of the cross, neither death nor failure have sting. They both have been overcome on the cross. (1 Cor. 15:54-55) We see fear as faith in the bad thing that is going to happen. Once I no longer fear failure, I step through my flesh by holding onto Jesus tightly. What seems like failure is endured to get me to the next place of trust and faith and helps open the doors for the call on my life so that what I was designed and created for would come about, along with the revelation necessary to bring it forth and begin walking it out. All of this comes through trust and faith in Jesus Christ and believing what he did on the cross was true.

As we embrace the truth that we cannot fail, from a value standpoint, this is a tool to overcome the flesh. I embrace this truth first by making the heartfelt decision to believe the truth of Jesus' shed blood on the cross. I make a conscious decision to step through potential failure, not to hide or avoid it. As I step into or towards the potential failures, I grab tightly onto Jesus, crying out and seeking his love and saving power. Eventually as I do this as a lifestyle, failure will neither have a grip nor sting on me. It is not about whether I fail or succeed according to some standard, but it is about trusting Jesus. Not anchoring my trust in people or what people think. Not worrying about what people think or trusting what people think as the rule of my value.

When I overcome failure, I have overcome my fear of what man or people think of me. Instead, I'm believing my value is anchored and I trust that my value is fully established, full and complete, through the shed blood of Jesus Christ on the cross.

My value can't get any better no matter what any person thinks or says. My value is already firmly established and I can't do anything to make it better. My value is anchored in the rock, Jesus Christ, and not in any person.

The second concept is I have to identify and crucify flesh,

understanding that God brings order through disorder. God is a God of order. We are created in his image, so we are created as a people of order. Our society values and focuses on order in a big way. If someone has the nicest, most orderly yard in the neighborhood, they are valued above others because of the order in their yard. People often can't function unless things are in order. People, even Christians, often put order as a top priority, the main thing in their life. Order becomes Lord or God in this scenario. They serve order first. When things are in order (1 Cor. 14:40), then they can focus on other things, including spiritual things.

The problem with this is God is order. And his order is not the same order that we often try to create. God actually will bring his order through our disorder, that we serve him and not order itself. The enemy will find ways to bring forth disorder in our life, especially as we seek to surrender our heart to God and crucify our flesh. It takes so much focus on order to create and keep my own personal order in my life. Once I let go of controlling my flesh, Satan and my surroundings release disorder in my life. I can anchor onto God and connect my heart in worship and love in the midst of the disorder. By doing this I'm letting go of my need to be in control and create my own order in my life. I re-anchor my hope in him instead of order and I learn to be content in all circumstances, even disorder.

I believe when I anchor in him instead of my need for order, God brings forth his order in my life, either through others or revelation in my heart totally embedded in his rest.

An example of disorder was when Jesus was in the midst of the storm. Not only was he at rest or peace in the storm, Jesus is able to bring his calm to the storms in our lives when we trust him and not in ourselves or our ability to create order.

Another way to crucify our flesh and begin trusting God and not our flesh is learning to walk in the self-control of the spirit instead of disciplining ourselves. We often try to improve ourselves by focusing our minds to discipline ourselves to make a change in our life to create more value in ourselves. We can be doing this while led by our mind. It is trying to create value in ourselves, to perform by creating change by rule or law, discipline or determination.

Our society, and even the church, has embraced this concept called discipline. With this model my mind takes headship or leadership place. There's no faith in purposing to perform through discipline. God is a performer. He created the heavens and the earth. We are created for a purpose, a design to do or perform out of God's plan for us. God performs out of who he is, not to get value. Our performance should come out of who we are, not out of trying to earn value.

Romans says anything short of faith is sin.

"..for whatever is not from faith is sin." Rom 14:23 NKJV

After all, one of the fruit of the Spirit is self-control. As believers, we do not discipline ourselves, we walk in the Spirit. By walking in the Spirit, we automatically have self-control, which is much better than discipline. We do not perform to get our value. (Gal.5:22,23)

CHAPTER 17

Planning By Faith Versus Budget Or Control

If Scripture tells us that anything other than faith is sin, do I just wait for God to move as I trust in my own plan? Or does God have a plan or vision for my life? Lots of believers are waiting for God to accomplish their plan or even his plan separate from their involvement.

You are right. God has a vision and a plan for each of us. But our heart not trusting and self-protecting gets in the way. If I trust him, I automatically hear his voice, or his language. "I do who I am" by trust or faith and his plan goes forth. I believe trust is the conduit that brings forth the exact revelation for the next step. I do not believe that we were created with the capacity to see all things or all the steps. The Scripture says we know in part.(1 Cor.13:9,12) By knowing in part, we have to rely on intimacy and connection, revelation and relationship with God to get us to the next step.

What God has been pursuing in all of us is trust. He laid the foundation with Jesus, our rock, our instrument of trust. Trust, or faith, releases the promises that brings forth God's plan - God's kingdom. To walk out this trust or faith (heart healing lays a foundation), we begin to start learning to communicate on a spirit level with God. Even though we are in the process of crucifying our flesh, we learn to plan and envision with God. We pray and learn to live more and more in his presence. We seek his plan and his will through prayer. God will begin to release this plan, this revelation, to us, not so that we can figure it out, but so we can pray into it and step towards it as he leads us. God uses our faith or trust to release his plans and his power that brings forth our purpose, our plan, and call on our life. It is unlike a budget where we are intellectually computing a plan or a vision, how to spend or not spend money to protect ourselves. God's plan requires faith to release his supernatural power, bringing forth his kingdom to change, as well as take over the world. God plans on taking over the world through our arms and legs. Although he owns the world, the enemy has made himself a ruler in the world and God plans to take back all the ground we gave Satan.

God is a planner. He releases impossible visions and plans that we have no ability to perform or do. That doesn't mean that, from time to time, we don't do those things we have the ability to do. These things are just not our focus. God's kingdom coming forth in our hearts and the hearts of men, that's God's focus. God may give us a large vision or a little vision, with little detail for our life, that we have no concept of how it could come forth. And even if he told us the larger vision, we just don't have the details of how it's to happen or come forth. We do not have the empowerment to make the vision happen. We're helpless to make the things happen that God has envisioned in our lives. We may feel like it isn't possible. And that is true while separate from God.

I seek to write these visions down as I get them, as well as the individual revelations that he gives me along the way. Writing down the visions God gives you is my suggestion to you. God is not going to give you these visions so you can go do them separate from him on your own. He is giving them to you so that you can pray into them. By faith, he leads you to do the steps that would often cause you to crucify your flesh, so that his empowerment can release the supernatural provision to bring forth his kingdom.

We are learning to trust him, not by our intellect, not by our carnal mind or our own understanding.

God wants us to love him based on <u>who he is</u> instead of what he does. By loving him based on who he is, we don't go through emotional ups and downs that destroy our trust and faith in him. We do not put God under a performance standard and love him based on what he does (he often doesn't do the things that we give him credit for anyway). By loving God based on his performance we take the lordship position as though we know better than God, that we have a better plan.

He wants us to love him based on who he is, not based on what he does. And out of that we don't get in the way of what he wants to release in our life.

If the plans and outcomes need to look like what I want them to be, or think they should be, I am making myself lord and I am seeking God to do my plan. God will not contribute to a plan where I am making myself lord. He loves me too much. He knows this only creates trauma and division in my heart and life. God will not support those things that harm me. God is a God of unity. He unifies hearts. He brings healing to hearts so that there can be unity and healing to the church, his bride, and so that he can bring unity and healing to the world. He is not willing that any shall perish.

> *"The Lord is not slack concerning His promise, as some count slackness, but is longsuffering toward us, not willing that any should perish but that all should come to repentance." 2 Pe 3:9 NKJV*

I'm not sure we fully understand what this means. I believe our revelation of his love for all of creation and all man is going to keep growing and multiplying in our hearts. The unity I have been talking of is brought forth by the ministry of reconciliation that he has given to us. (Col.1:10) We are called to the ministry of reconciliation. Reconciliation will restore all things to whole, to his design and creation. He has called us, as believers, to reconcile Jesus to the world, to bring unity and wholeness. He's called the church to reconcile Jesus to each other. This also means bringing unity or wholeness by "living in the Spirit."

He has also called the spirit side of our heart that is led by his spirit to reconcile Jesus to the broken part of our heart. This will bring unity and wholeness to our heart. This last statement about our hearts is a foundational statement. Because as we see reconciliation with Jesus in our hearts, in the hearts of men, the kingdom will automatically come forth in unity and wholeness according to the fullness of God in his vision and plan. Out of this restoration, the DNA will be restored in all of us and in the world. Out of this I believe order will be established physically (no more sickness or disease), emotionally and spiritually. The enemy will have no place. We will walk in our true identity, collectively in perfect cadence. Out of this true identity we speak, we will create according to God's visions and purposes and plans.

Reconciliation will restore all things to whole, to his design and creation. He has called us, as believers, to reconcile Jesus to the world, to bring unity and wholeness.

CHAPTER 18

Unity of Heart, Church and World

God is in the process of restoring all things to his perfect plan and order and design, which will automatically bring forth unity in all creation, including all men. It originally broke when Adam and Eve fell away from trusting God and decided to self-protect and become their own protectors. They believed the lie of Satan over God's truth. Man has been trying to bring restoration to himself ever since, even though he is not capable of restoring himself. He has no ability to restore himself. His quest to restore himself separate from God is unbelief, which manifests itself in self-protection, self-focus, or "my will be done."

This self-focus catapults us into divisiveness, offense, and broken hearts. Hearts broken and flesh are at war with unity and

God's truth, creating its own truth and its own understanding. Carnal truth is established in this through what Scripture calls the "natural man." As a result of this carnal truth man is plagued with fear of loss and inability to trust, not only God but anyone. We may think we trust certain people in our lives. Or do we? If we do not trust God to protect us, we truly can't trust people. In all of this confusion, our hearts are broken, the church is broken (the bride), the world, its people, are broken, and all creation is broken. When Father God looks at all of this, he sees the truth and not the lie or the deception that it is broken. He sees it as it is, as the original creation fully restored. This restoration is the truth, "the real". What we see is the deception. And as long as we see and believe that the deception is "the real", our faith is in the deception which propels it to look and act as truth and reality.

Faith releases God's promises but it also releases whatever our hearts believe in, including this deception. As long as we believe and see the world as broken, its brokenness will have power to multiply because we believe the deception to the point of it manifesting in our lives physically. We take on the identity of the deception. We give life to the deception. And as we speak into this deception as though it is the real, we prophetically propel it forward. We propel forward death and deception.

If I speak a word into the deception, I come into agreement with the deception and prophetically release it into my surroundings and the world for all creation and all matter to record.

Did you know matter has memory? And it's recording your words for all eternity. No worries, speak the truth. Believe the truth. If you robbed a bank yesterday, does that make you a bank robber? Most people would say yes, I physically robbed a bank, so there is no denying I am a bank robber. The proof is that the physical bank robbery took place and it fully is verifiable in the physical realm.

As long as I believe this truth and speak into the truth, I take on the identity that I am a bank robber and I will continue to rob banks.

Satan's lie is that God does not fully love us and that he rejects us. As long as we believe this, we will constantly seek to create value in ourselves through that self-focus, "my will be done" lifestyle that brings forth the dominance of the flesh and the lies.

The truth is God fully loves me unconditionally and if I rob a bank, I do it because I do not know his love. If I don't know his love, I can't know my true identity. If I know the fullness of God's unconditional love, I know my true identity and I can't sin. It's impossible. I can't rob a bank.

Our identity is that we are fully righteous, being fully and unconditionally loved by God. People sin because they think they are who the devil says they are. If their flesh or broken heart believes that's who they are and because their flesh dominates and they spend lots of time in their flesh, they take on the identity of their flesh as the reality. The truth is they are not who Satan and their flesh, in partnership with their broken heart, says they are. They are who God says they are. No matter what sin they have just done, they are righteous, they are holy, they are who God says they are. We are who God says we are, not the mistakes and the sins that we've done. When I believe this, I will automatically walk it out. My spirit connected to God's spirit knows the truth but the flesh believes the lie.

It is important to make God's truth my reality. It is important not to make my physical reality truth. That is believing the lie. This is why Scripture says those things seen are temporal but those things unseen are eternal.

> *"...while we do not look at the things which are seen, but at the things which are not seen. For the things which are seen are temporary, but the things which are not seen are eternal." 2 Cor 4:18 NKJV*

This concept of making God's truth my reality is not only true with our individual life, but is true with the life of the church as well as the life of the world, including our individual country.

I begin to speak and believe life into myself, into the church, and into the world by making decisions to do so and empowering those decisions by beginning to live in the Spirit, constantly, totally dependent on God's power and not mine. Those that walk in the spirit will not obey the desires of the flesh. (Gal 5:16) Those that walk in the spirit are sons of God. (Rom.8:14) As I walk in the spirit, unity comes forth, not self-protection, on every level of creation. My heart becomes One Whole Heart. The church becomes one body. The world and creation unifies into all that God created it to be. This revelatory Living is walking and living out of God's perfect design, order, and DNA and out of this faith <u>All Creation Becomes Whole</u>.

The question is, what does that look like as we move towards that? Individually it means God is my Protector in everything. I embrace the concept that, "if I end up homeless, naked, without food, totally humiliated or even dead, I'm going to trust you, God. No matter what I'm going through, I'm going to trust you, God. I have nothing to lose. My life has been paid for, that I can physically die but I can't actually die. My life is eternal in you, Jesus. I can't fail because you, God, paid that no one can accuse me. Therefore, I can't lose value so I don't have to protect my reputation. Actually, no one has anything they can do to harm me or take from me that you have not overcome, Jesus. I have nothing to protect, nothing to lose. You have paid for it all, Jesus." This trust is a sign of my heart being unified as I fully become the spirit man that God created me to be. I live and walk in the spirit constantly.

When we do this collectively and in unity in the church, our churches will become churches of unity in the Spirit. We will walk in perfect harmony in the body of Christ. No longer will man be self-protecting and building a church and fighting one another in divisiveness. But we will see each other as part of God's church, for who they are, having open hands towards each other with people and resources, as God moves believers from church to church to ministry according to his plan.

Our hearts will be to release people into their call and their destiny and their true identity. God has one church but many parts of the body and we do not have the capacity, revelation or ability to orchestrate its function or design. Only God can do this as we walk individually and corporately as the church in total dependence on him. Step by step, breath by breath. Anytime we think we can do this based on our own understanding, we are back into the natural man and the flesh and self-protecting. God created us individually and corporately for full dependence on him, that he is involved with every step as we continually walk in the spirit. As we overcome the flesh through his power and connection and intimacy, we automatically overcome the devil and the world and live out of God's Spirit. Out of all this unity, the world and creation will come in alignment with God's design.

"For the earnest expectation of the creation eagerly waits for the revealing of the sons of God." Rom 8:19 NKJV

CHAPTER 19

The Hard Walk of Crucifying the Flesh

The One Whole Heart healing process includes numerous two-hour sessions during which God has been giving us the opportunity to release incredible healing to the hearts of his precious children. Hearts are opened and softened and just excited to walk out the call and the destiny of God. The One Whole Heart healing process creates trust and vision that comes in connection with Jesus, as we are further learning the language of God through healing.

For a person to live out who they really are, their true identity, the healing of the heart is very necessary. Without healing, we live out of self-protection and pleasing people and don't know who we really are. It would be great if the adversary just gave up at the point of completion of sessions. It normally does not work this way. These incredible life-changing breakthroughs lay a foundation through softening the heart and taking ground back from the enemy to begin to crucify the flesh.

Scripture says no man tames the tongue (Which could be interpreted as the tongue being a type of flesh). The tongue/ flesh is wicked beyond all things.

> *"The heart is deceitful above all things, And desperately wicked; Who can know it?" Jer 17:9 NKJV*

> *"But no man can tame the tongue. [It is] an unruly evil, full of deadly poison." Jas 3:8 NKJV*

God is the only empowerment to overcome the flesh. We must learn to forgive people and empower God the moment we have offense in our thoughts. We need to recognize we are offended and begin to eliminate the patterns that we have walked out for years. These patterns used to be connected to the roots which have been removed through the healing process. God's goodness has dealt with those roots.

The enemy looks to help create new offenses so that he can reconnect the old patterns to the new offense. It is Satan's effort to maintain his stronghold and keep this ground. If we forgive and repent and do the whole-heart process called *whole-hearting ourselves,* we are able to disconnect old patterns. Then the enemy does not have a way to pull us in the flesh through these old patterns and to reconnect them. Patterns can be those places of self-protection the broken part of the heart formed out of the ingredients of the heart. These patterns are negative emotions that show up. Some of these include the mind beginning to race, anxiety, fear and anger. It is the same patterns that we were used to having in the past.

For example, you fell out of the car when you were two years old but this event or memory has been reconciled and healed. When it had first happened, your heart went into overload and broke. When it broke, you formed a protection system that included anxiety, fear, worry, anger and confusion, among others. Let's say you always started to feel these feelings when you were around an automobile that someone else was driving. Or it could be other instances when your dad failed to protect you. Through healing of your heart, you reconcile the memory and other memories related to your dad. Jesus brought his love into the broken part of your heart in this and healing fully came forth as a result. You began to have a new love and trust for both Dad and God. From this healing you are feeling the intimacy and presence of God and the Holy Spirit, in a deeper and deeper way. The self-protection pattern that I referred to previously of the racing thoughts, anxiety, fear and anger is now dead or dying.

After this, the adversary may align and create situations, perhaps starting with your husband or your wife, to cause events that don't protect you and put you in harm's way in the family car. When these situations first arrive, your heart is at peace, but a thought comes to your mind quietly. You begin to think that your spouse does not care about you enough to avoid the situation that just put you at risk while they were driving. The thought was quiet, without feeling, so you ignore it. Several more thoughts continue to come along with feelings that are slight and you begin to feel a tiny bit of tension or sadness. The feelings continue to escalate. You notice other events arise as your heart, believing the lie about your value, draws on these new situations. Eventually, even though your root trauma with your dad was reconciled, Satan is able to reconnect the old pattern, including the escalated feelings of fear, anxiety and anger to these new events and new offenses. It almost feels like the old pattern. It feels like it's still in place, connected to the old Dad trauma.

The enemy will also bring thoughts of what happened with Dad to try to trigger your mind into trying to self-protect. While this is happening, both your mind and your emotions are escalating in numbers and intensity of thoughts. In order to solve the problem and self-protect, your flesh brings on more partner emotions with deeper intensity.

The key to all this is unforgiveness. When we take up a new offense, it allows old patterns to have life.

We teach a process called *whole-hearting yourself* that is a forgiveness process during which we get permission from the broken part of our heart so that God's love can enter. When God's love enters the broken part of our heart and empowers the forgiveness at a heart and feeling level it will bring us right back in the spirit. We need to learn to live out of the spirit all the time.

As we whole-heart ourselves continuously when offenses arise, eventually the enemy stops trying and the old patterns go away. You can find the *One Whole Heart process* or *whole-hearting yourself* on the One Whole Heart website labeled "Whole Hearting Yourself Circles." As of writing this, that particular tool was on the very front page of the website www.onewholeheartministry.com. We also have 4 x 5 index cards available to help implement this dependency on God's protection and power.

As the patterns go away, there's less and less flesh to pull us out of the spirit. The less flesh means that there's less of a pull to pull us out of the spirit. We become less and less double-minded.

"...he is a double-minded man, unstable in all his ways." Jas 1:8 NKJV

When we learn to whole-heart ourselves and get back in the spirit right away, this helps us create the lifestyle of walking in the spirit. If this was all it took to walk out our call and our destiny, it would be difficult, but much simpler than what it takes to eliminate the flesh that wants to dominate in our lives. It is very, very important to seek deep intimacy with the Lord and total dependency on him during this time, really from this time on, through both individual and corporate intimacy and constantly clinging to God.

When we are going through the process of seeking healing for our hearts, we often just want to be fixed and live happily ever after. Healing the heart is really not about getting fixed. It's about healing of our heart so that we can become who we really are. Who we are is separate from our self-protection, which creates a new paradigm, bringing us into totally new revelation of how to live life. We can't go through sessions and then think we can go back and live the lifestyle that we're used to with the old man, the natural man, and expect lasting change. The enemy will be able to reconquer ground. Fortunately, as healing comes, so does revelation and empowerment to step into a new paradigm of the Spirit (the Spirit man) along with the eventual lifestyle change we were created for. We were created to bring forth the Kingdom. We are about the Kingdom. With our hearts healed,

Whole Heart Yourself

Five Type of Offense

1. Blame*

2. Rejection*

3. Fear

4. "Fixing" someone

5. Judgement

*Partners with anger and confusion

 # 1
Forgive & Repent

 # 2
Establish people protector
(me at this place and all the times I've been hurt like this before)

 # 3
Feeling protectors
First group: anger, confusion, any type of offense thought or feeling that comes with it

Asking Jesus to come close, then all the way in

 # 4
Feeling protectors
Second group: all other current feelings and self-protection

Asking Jesus to come close, then all the way in

Asking Jesus to come close to me in all the times I've been hurt like this before, then all the way in

Look on our website under Mentoring Videos for the teaching video
"Whole Heart Yourself Circles" **www.onewholeheartministry.com**

I. Identify you are offended by type of thoughts, from: Blame, Rejection, Fear, "Fixing" someone, and Judgement.

II. Forgive and repent for the offense and the times the person did it.

III. Place offenses that have been identified* with anger and confusion and speak to all of them asking permission first for God to come close.

Example –You identified blame and rejection. You say: *"Blame, rejection, anger and confusion, you are a broken part of my heart. It does not work for you to do what you are doing to try to protect. Would it be OK if Jesus comes close?"*

You wait and listen for a thought that says "Yes" and you will feel God's presence. Then you say: *"Would it be OK for God/Jesus to come all the way in?"* You will hear or sense a "Yes" and feel the peace of God's presence.

Note:*When you are speaking to those protectors you have identified and you have some feeling you are experiencing at the same time, like sadness, doubt, shame, guilt, lust, anxiety, etc., you should speak to those feelings also. This applies to both circle 3 and/or 4.

IV. With circle 4, talk to any other protectors you haven't identified that are left. You do not need to identify protectors. You also can talk with any additional feelings that you feel while doing circle 4.

Example: You say, *"I'm talking to all other self-protection that is around in this plus shame (or what negative feelings are present). You are a broken part of my heart. It does not work for you to do what you are doing to try to protect. Would it be OK for Jesus to come close?"*

Wait to sense or feel a "Yes" and God's peace will show up.

You then say: *"Would it be OK for Jesus to come all the way in?"* You then go back to circle 2. You say: *"I am talking to myself and the hurt I experienced in this situation(s). Would it be OK if Jesus comes close to me in this situation?"*

You will sense a "Yes" and feel more of God's peace.

You then say: *"Would it be OK for Jesus to come all the way into me in this situation?"*

You will sense a "Yes" and feel God's peace.

After all this I like to send my heart to heaven and worship God.

Mentoring videos and more information can be found at
www.onewholeheartministry.com

Pushes and Pulls

Pushes

You ask God: *Father God, if I do _____, how am I going to feel?* If you feel negative emotions or even a feeling of being pushed a direction, you go the opposite direction. That is your flesh pushing. (God will not push or pull.) Go the opposite direction your flesh wants you to go.

Trip Example: You are trying to determine whether God wants you to take a particular trip, if this trip is led by God's plans. You ask: "Father God, if I take this trip to Cambodia, how am I going to feel?"

If you feel negative emotions or resistant feelings, your flesh is trying to protect or keep you from taking the trip. You could feel anxiety, fear, or resistant feelings that are making you feel "No, don't go." These feelings are flesh. You need to grab onto Jesus by asking, *"Help me, Jesus"* and focusing on Jesus and take the trip to crucify your flesh. While on the trip your flesh will continue to show up in negative feelings as well as negative thoughts. If you cry out to Jesus and focus on him while this is going on, your flesh will eventually get weaker and go away and the trust you have in Jesus will increase.

Pulls

You ask God: *Father God, if I don't _____, how am I going to feel?*

If you have negative emotions or even a feeling of being pulled a direction, that is your flesh pulling. (God will not push or pull.) Whatever direction your flesh wants you to go, you go the other direction to crucify your flesh.

Ice Cream Example: You ask: "Father God, if I don't stop and have ice cream, how am I going to feel?" You feel your flesh pulling you. "I want ice cream" is what you sense that is hard to resist. You call out to God, "Jesus, help me" as you drive by the ice cream place and crucify your flesh.

It is possible to have a push and pull happen at the same time going opposite directions. If that happens, go the opposite direction of the one that shows up timing-wise first, and when that dies and loses its strength, go the other direction and crucify the flesh the other direction.

Mentoring videos and more information can be found at
www.onewholeheartministry.com

Structure Tool Short Form

1. Identify the negative thoughts or feelings.

2. You say: *"Father God, show me a picture of me as a person in the Spirit, you in me and me in you."* As the picture comes to your imagination, remember it because you are going to use it several times.

Go through your imagination in the picture of you in the Spirit to the place inside where the negative thoughts or feelings are. It may be a picture of you at an earlier age or a feeling or you sense where that place is. If you are not sure, ask God to show you where it is.

When you get to that place(s), you in the Spirit (picture) say: *"I'm sorry if I hurt you or did not listen to your voice. You are a broken part of my heart. We are meant to be together, not separate. I love you."*

Then embrace or hug that place in your imagination. You are speaking (nonverbal in your thoughts) to that place(s) with the negative thoughts or feelings are as though it was a person. There may be several places. Keep looking or asking God to show you until there are none left and speak to each one with the same above words.

Do not get into any other conversation with those places because it will pull you into the carnal mind.

You have just completed the short form of reconciling your broken heart by the Spirit side of your heart.

Mentoring videos and more information can be found at
www.onewholeheartministry.com

Whole Heart the Mind and Body

Before you speak to the mind we're going to speak to the places of overload from the mind, including:

Void, empty places; Numbness; Headaches; Disconnectedness.

Tell those places, *"Void, empty places; Numbness; Headaches; Disconnectedness, you weren't created to do what you're doing. Is it all right if Jesus comes close to those places?"*

Tell those places, *"I know you're tired and exhausted, but you actually get in the way of Jesus coming into the mind to bring rest, so that you don't have to do what you're doing. It doesn't work."*

1. *"Is it all right if Jesus comes close?"*

2. *"Can God come fill any empty void and saturate every place? All the way in?"*

Speak to the mind:

"I'm going to tell you that the mind was never created to fix the heart."

"The more times you hear an answer, you have more questions."

"The more questions you have, the more hopeless you are."

"It's like a deep, dark, black pit, never-ending hopelessness."

"It just doesn't work. But if you let Jesus come close, you're going to be able to rest. He'll show you what you were created for. Would that be OK?"

You sense and feel the thoughts calming.

"Is it all right if Jesus brings the mind that's trying to fix the heart totally into himself?"

You're looking for a Yes.

Go to the next page to whole heart the body.

Mentoring videos and more information can be found at
www.onewholeheartministry.com

Whole Heart the Body

Speak to the Body

"I'm talking to the top of my head, to the bottom of my feet, even the ends of my fingers -- every cell and every atom -- even those that don't trust God."

Say: *"You were never created to do what you do separate from God. Would it be OK if Jesus would bring every cell and atom all the way into him?"*

Wait for a feeling of Yes.

Speak to the Body section by section (do in 3 sections):

Focus on each part likes it's a person. You will hear Yes and feel God's presence come like a "whoosh." <u>Go till all the parts are done in all 3 sections of your body.</u> As you choose the parts of the body, if you go too large a part, you won't feel His presence as much; if you go too small, it could take a very long time. You choose.

<u>Do section 1 until complete, then go to section 2.</u>

1. Top of your head, shoulders, to the end of your fingers. Part by part ask, *"Is it OK if Jesus comes?"* Start at the face and ask your face, *"Is it OK if Jesus comes?"*

<u>Do section 2 till completion, then go to section 3.</u>

2. Top of your shoulder to the waist. Speak to your organs if you wish also.

<u>Do section 3 till completion.</u>

3. Waist down to the bottom of the feet.

"Is it OK if Jesus comes and saturates the whole body?"

Body Position-do not reposition before, during, or after till you come out of disappearing with the Holy Spirit.

Mentoring videos and more information can be found at
www.onewholeheartministry.com

God will bring forth our calling, which does not look like self-protection but looks like the Kingdom.

One way this happens is when I begin to seek my identity and my purpose by starting to overcome my flesh as a continuous lifestyle, crucifying my flesh or overcoming my flesh on a regular basis. God is all about crucifying my flesh because it eliminates the enemy's license to control and lead me to believe his word instead of God's word. God's truth is about the Lord's unconditional love and his shed blood on the cross to verify this love. It's my flesh that gets in the way of me trusting God and being exactly who he created me to be and his Kingdom going forth in my life.

As I step in the opposite direction from where my flesh wants to take me, my mind will bring forth thoughts of self-protection and condemnation. That is because flesh, as it's dying, shows up and even intensifies to take control, especially when it is trying to keep from dying. As I war against my flesh, I have no power to overcome my flesh, so the way to overcome the flesh is to grab onto God tightly, emotionally, seeking his help, and seeking my heart to connect, worship, and seek and cry out to him sincerely.

> *"But no man can tame the tongue. [It is] an unruly evil, full of deadly poison." Jas 3:8 NKJV*

> *(With this verse I am identifying that the tongue as one type of flesh and just as the tongue can not be tamed neither can the flesh in its entirety.)*

All this re-anchors me from looking to people and myself to protect me, to looking to God and him alone to overcome my flesh. He is my Protector, him alone.

Often we bring our problems to people and try to get advice in the mind on an intellectual level. That doesn't work. We always end up with more and more problems. People do not have the ability to fix our heart. We can't protect ourselves. God is our Protector. He alone can protect and comfort us.

The other problem with going to people is verbalizing our problems. As we are speaking out our problems to people, this can often release the faith in the "power of the problems" and cause them to multiply. The mind also magnifies and partners racing thoughts with the problem. When we do come up with a solution of our own understanding, we anchor our trust in either the solution or the people connected to the solution. If we look to God to be the solution through intimately anchoring in him to have his way, our flesh will surely die and trust will open doors to what God wants to release in our lives, in the way he wants to release it. He is Lord and our loving faithful Father. Instead of looking to people and speaking out death as we speak into the problems, we begin to learn to go to him and seek him intimately for the solution.

One of the pitfalls of stepping through our flesh continuously as we seek to have God crucify our flesh is that the flesh fights hard through thoughts and feelings. It is common, while stepping through this, to get overwhelmed with flesh or grief as this flesh-dying process goes on. You can begin to take on the identity of the flesh you are feeling, even to the point of depression and despair.

Our flesh dies hard. This is a very difficult process. My suggestion is to be focused on the forgiveness with whole-hearting yourself while you maintain as first priority seeking deep intimacy with God individually and corporately. Do not let the flesh take control and cause isolation. We need believers around us that have walked through this and can encourage us to keep our eyes on Jesus.

People, through their testimony, can encourage and speak revelation into us about the process we are going through. It instills hope and understanding that we are on track to crush the flesh. When other believers have walked through this death process and have revelation of the process, they can encourage those stepping into it. The devil wants us to isolate and begin to use our flesh to attack our identity. Our victory in this is the flesh dying and all the hopes connected to the flesh. You are re-anchoring your hope in Jesus Christ and his shed blood on the cross and out of this will come your true identity.

CHAPTER 20

Faith-Filled Structure

As our flesh dies, we often get stuck in the liberty of faith and don't realize God uses structure and authority to crucify our flesh and bring forth his Kingdom. We were told and even discovered that God's presence feels like peace. So many believers will seek that peace, not realizing that they have to at the same time crucify their flesh, which does not feel like peace.

Although God's love and presence feels like peace, we also need to be stepping through our flesh and crucifying our flesh at the same time, which feels like flesh and doesn't feel like peace.

We can go to church and worship and get into the spirit and survive by seeking the deep and often intimate feelings of these events or conferences, without taking the life steps to crucify our flesh.

As we talked about earlier, the flesh must die that I can walk out my calling and release my true identity to the world. As I am crucifying my flesh, this brings the feeling of death of my flesh forward because I am no longer seeking to perform and do things to get value. Instead, so much death can show up that I feel overwhelmed and helpless even to do the smallest tasks, let alone an overwhelming project, so I can get stuck running and hiding from tasks.

As I crucify the flesh, there is a drive by my flesh to isolate myself and not step through my flesh and step into these value seeking performance tasks I'm talking about or even seek to walk in sin or offense (anger) to feel justified. However if I press through my fighting flesh and grab unto Jesus, death of the flesh will eventually come.

This death brings me to a completely different place. This place has some connection and some intimacy with God even though my hopelessness can get in the way at times.

The Christian walk can seem so hard because I die to my flesh and let go of my own performance agenda and ambitions to surrender to God. As I do this surrender It seems like I don't do much or know anything. This truly feels like death. I feel like I don't bring anything to the table, I'm helpless, no gifts or abilities. Death of our flesh is a process. This Process takes time as God builds in me both patience and trust.

As I grab onto God intimately in this time, eventually I will overcome by the blood of the Lamb (clinging to Jesus). This victory moves me to a new season for my flesh to die to new areas of self protection (justification). I believe though, during all of these moves of God in our lives, it is healthy to minister healing to ourselves clinging to Jesus. It also is healthy during these times to minister healing to others through prayer and prophetic ministry as you press in and continue to learn the language of the Holy Spirit and crucify your flesh. As we give away what we have, God multiplies it inside of us and we feel the joy of the Lord more abundant. This joy helps us walk through the process of crucifying our flesh. But if I isolate, the joy of the Lord is not in the midst of isolation for protection. With this isolation the carnal flesh with raising thoughts and offenses are dominating my life.

What God wants to move us into next is the unraveling we talked about earlier. I believe God is a God of structure. The Bible is a structure God uses to teach us his voice even through our mind and by the law initially. Eventually he moves us out of the law into the spirit. This is just like the pattern he established moving from the law of the Old Testament to Jesus and the Holy Spirit of God in the New Testament. What God does is bring forth structure, not under the law, but by the Spirit. At this place we have been talking about getting victory by stepping through the death of performing for value. We feel stuck. This place represents an ideal time for God to move us into structure in our lives, to pull us out of the place of no or little vision or plan. It is this structure that helps bring forth the Kingdom, the vision, the plan by faith and serves as a tool to crush the flesh. Structure can look like a schedule of appointments or a vision of specific times to take small steps. It is accompanied by prayer to step through those things or tasks God wants us to overcome in our lives, in partnership with him. It is these structures, plans and visions which I have to grab onto at this place because it is my relationship and intimacy with God that keeps these structures in place not my own strength or ability. The devil, through my flesh, wants me to abandon these structures and be without direction or functionality. Knowing that God gave me the structure and the plan and the vision, I hang onto it because the devil wants to steal it and use my flesh to do it. The enemy does this just like the attempt by Sanballat in Nehemiah was used to discourage Nehemiah. (Neh. 6:14)

What if we don't have a plan from God? Then look for a structure, a schedule, or a task to step towards by his lead and his Spirit. Grab onto whatever he gives you and don't let go. The schedule should walk out one day at a time, one moment, not looking back or projecting forward. You may have a month or several months of appointments, but we walk it out one moment at a time and one day at a time.

If there is a task to overcome, then don't try to analyze the task with your carnal mind by looking back or projecting forward. That is flesh. You simply pray and take the little steps God has you take one step at a time. Grab onto God and cry out to him and let him orchestrate the steps as he leads you step by step, through the overwhelming impossibility because you, at the time, have no capacity to get through separate from him. He will do all the heavy lifting in this. He shoulders the project, not you. The assignment is his job to complete. He has ownership. You just continue to pray and make the small steps that may seem at times big because your flesh does not want to make these steps. By making these steps, the flesh goes through a dying process.

An example of all this in my life was when I owed that massive amount of money I talked about before and eventually built the house, which was all done by this little step-by-step unraveling process with no debt. Going from owing maybe a million or more dollars to having no debt was impossible in my mind and my heart.

At that time, the Lord also told me to go back into the real estate business. My flesh certainly did not want to do that. I did not trust my flesh after coming out of all the years of greed and all that went with that. I had a conviction in my heart to never let my heart get back into that place of greed. So the last thing I wanted to do was to go back into real estate and deal with the greed or the money aspect again.

That is the very thing God had me do. He put me right back smack in the middle of that. By his power and my dependency on him, I overcame my fears instead of running and hiding from them. He also put me in a real estate office that had several of the same people I worked with during the residential part of the business failure and I felt humiliated and ashamed to be seen by them. I was doing commercial real estate in a large residential real estate office, so I had to overcome my fears of even walking into the office each day and seeing the people and feelings of extreme embarrassment just getting through the door.

I remember the extreme fear, anxiety, worry and sadness I had to step through each day. I would call on God constantly by saying over and over "Jesus help me."

The Lord also had me cold-call a three-inch thick directory of retailers each day, from three to six hours a day. Each call I made, I would be extremely fearful of rejection. So before I would make each call, I would pray and grab onto Jesus and then make the call.

I had lots of tears and lots of emotions, but this exercise of stepping through my flesh and crushing my flesh worked quite well to overcome these fears and anchor my hope in Jesus. I took these small steps day by day, moment by moment, to overcome my flesh and move with God as he unraveled the beginning of my call, my destiny. The flesh has to die.

I had a structure, a schedule and a plan in all of this I knew God wanted me to step into. I did not have vision or direction at the time, except to step through the office doors and make the calls, which was also very hard because I was stepping into a new industry. I had done residential real estate but that was nothing like commercial real estate. I had no one to teach me, so I learned as I made the frightful Real Estate cold calls.

I had no vision or understanding of what to expect or hope for from day to day financially. It was all commission based. I did learn in this process that commercial real estate was dramatically harder to break through and remain in financially than residential. But God gave me the breakthrough.

And again my advice at this stage is stepping through and crucifying the flesh. Don't look back to the past mistakes with your mind, as though you have to overcome on your own. Don't project forward and figure out outcomes based on reasons or scenarios. Do not put your hope in outcomes. Put your hope in Jesus and his shed blood on the cross. Looking back or projecting forward in these examples are both thought processes that are out of the carnal mind. Take it moment by moment, step by step, totally dependent on Jesus, connecting to his heart and getting your full identity out of his victory and his shed blood and not from your performance.

So step. Step by step, moment by moment, not looking back and not looking forward. Walk motivated by his love in the spirit. This will bring forth his plan for your life. Money or getting value from people or any other type of self-protection are dysfunctional motivators.

CHAPTER 21

Learning Directly From God - God is Our Teacher

God is our teacher. I will teach you. (Ex ,4:12,

1 John 2:27)

I really believe that as we move into the place of deeper trust of Father God, this opens the door so that he can release to us the revelations we already carry, that are part of our DNA. In this, he begins to teach us directly. As we look to him to teach us, he releases the personal revelations that we were created to carry according to his design and plan for us. These revelations are for us to connect intimately with him and walk out the true purpose and calling on our life. No one else carries the revelations we carry to bring forth the Kingdom on this planet.

All people carry unique revelations. Collectively, as we walk in them, the Kingdom of God will fully come forth supernaturally by the power of God partnered with our trust and our faith.

God chose to bring forth his Kingdom in partnership or unity with us. He could have brought forth a Kingdom on his own because he has all the power and dominion, but he chose to bring it forth in unity with us. God releasing his power and love while we release our trust, wrapped in his love - out of this we release his love to the world.

Love is the nature and foundation of God's Kingdom coming forth. Trust is the principal conduit to release his love. His Kingdom is of righteousness, peace and joy in the Holy Spirit. Thank you, Father God, for your love.

I believe in the process of moving towards getting more and deeper revelation, and intimacy from God directly. It is important to make the decision to focus and move in that direction. There are numbers of incredible men and women of God with deep revelations from God that continue to help us grow towards God and his love. I am very appreciative that God has brought forth these wonderful people to help move us closer to him.

The vision of a preacher, or a teacher, or evangelist, or apostle of the Lord is to point God's people to him, to receive directly from him, to receive not only love from God but also revelation. That revelation comes forth in the mind of our spirit or the mind of our heart. Our job is to propel each other through love to receive directly from the Father. We are to encourage, edify, build up, speaking the real truth, which are those things that are often unseen, those eternal things. Those things include speaking life into each other based on who we are, not based on that which we do when we trip or fall, in this seen world that is temporal.

Speak the truth in love. The truth is always based on our true identity. The truth is based on the things that are unseen that will materialize, as we trust God and begin to walk in who we really are.

Through that unraveling, walking in the spirit, in full partnership with God, we co-create with God to bring forth his Kingdom. He truly is in partnership with us, going to take over the headship and the future, as all creation turns to trust him.

I remember there was a time in my life when God moved me and my family to a church that did not operate in charisma or the visible movement of the Holy Spirit. The church was a large body that functioned a lot out of intellectual knowledge and a performance mentality, often using performance to gain value as a body. God deeply loved and loves this body of believers, both individually and corporately. The dilemma I had was the things I had experienced spiritually was not understood by this body or the pastoral staff. At the time, God was moving in my heart to teach me a deep understanding of how the payment on the cross was full and complete, that we didn't and couldn't pay for or get value by anything we did and that he already fully paid for and established our value. In other words, the grace and the mercy of God was being established in my heart. It was demonstrated, being lived out in my life.

I believe that God wanted me at this church. He had told my wife and I, as we came in agreement, to go to this church. He had called me to this church for this season.

We need to be at the place or the church that God calls us to and not be where our mind or our own understanding directs us to be. Sheep often get fat. They get fed too much. God has a plan. Let's go with his plan. We don't leave where we're at (normally) because we are not getting fed or we are offended. We move as God has us move, not because our flesh would have us go.

If we are offended, almost always our flesh is in this, pulling or pushing us to make a move. If we follow our flesh in this, we strengthen and empower our flesh and we surely will find circumstances like we left at the next church or ministry. These circumstances will keep following us around until we, by the blood of the Lamb, overcome them. In other words, we stay in the midst of the difficult circumstances and make God our Protector and hold onto him tight as we cry out to him. He will overcome by his supernatural power and build trust in our hearts.

This trust does not come by us vocalizing our offenses and creating division and faction. It comes between us and God directly, looking to him for the breakthrough and not people.

When I vocalize the problems, I multiply them and give life to them and speak life and faith into them. Everything in my life is between me and God. Out of that reconciliation of my heart, I pour out God's unconditional love to people based on who they are, not what they are doing. What they are doing may be out of their flesh, their broken heart and reflect Satan's lie or deception, not who they really are. If I focus or speak into this deception, it brings faith into it, which prophetically propels it forward in their life and mine. I may gently, verbally acknowledge it as the deception. I move right into the truth about the person or the church. For example, "You are not a person that would speak this way about Pastor John. I know it came out, but that's not who you are. You are an incredible gift-ed encourager filled with God's love." This is an example of speaking to someone who just criticized the pastor.

We need to overcome. We are overcomers. I am not say-ing there is never a time to leave a church or ministry when there are difficult circumstances. If the person's maturity level does not afford them the ability or the support to overcome, or there are physical or sexual perversions, or twisted situations in the church - by all means leave. But really, if we can seek to be led by the Lord in all things, not people, or mental concepts, or rules, but being led by the Lord - this is our safest place. God is our Protector, not us and not people.

While I was at this church, I was definitely not getting fed as we talk about growing or getting fed. But I knew this was where God wanted me, so I stayed, prayed for the people, loved the people. I would spend hours a day getting fed by the Lord directly. I believe this period of time was instrumental in me learning to look to the Lord and to get my revelations directly from him, not people.

If God had put me in a church with a powerful or charis-matic pastor or pastoral staff and culture, maybe I still would be looking to people instead of God for my revelations. There is a time to begin to look to get our revelations directly from God. It does not mean that you will never receive from people. You will receive from people always through the filter of God's Spirit.

I am thankful for those people that have given and re-leased revelation into my heart, the pastors and teachers. I am very thankful. However, there is a time that God wants to speak directly into your heart and give you the revelations directly. Often those are revelations that go beyond the intellect, go beyond what people think, and really may even seem twisted or strange to people, but you know they're true and you know they're right because they came directly from your Father.

CHAPTER 22

Two Gospels

There are really only two gospels that all people live their lives by; all people. Often People think that these gospels have to do with mental understanding of believing or not believing. An example would be if my mind has a cognitive agreement that Jesus is God that is one gospel. If I don't believe that Jesus is God in my mind that is the second gospel. If one believes or if one doesn't believe, in my mind, that would be the two gospels. My thoughts differ from this a bit because our carnal minds can believe in lots of concepts that we don't live out and don't demonstrate in our life. If I told you that it was important for me to run ten miles every day or I was going to get extremely sick and die. I verbally told you I had this belief. If you watched me in my life and I never go out and ran each day. There is a problem that what I say and what I do are not consistent. I am not doing what I am saying in this area of my life. I would suggest I do not believe in my heart that I need to run ten miles a day to protect my health, otherwise, I would go running every day.

This understanding says that there are times that I have mind concepts in my carnal mind and even profess them but I do not really believe them in my heart. It demonstrates a difference between having a concept in my carnal mind and believing in my heart.

If I believe in Jesus and his shed blood on the cross in my heart, it will translate to love in my heart. The two gospels I refer to are : (1) the gospel of performance by the law and (2) the gospel of God's grace and mercy that Jesus has paid with his shed blood on the cross for all our past, present and future sins or mistakes and through faith in what he did on the cross actually happened.

These two gospels are the gospel of the law in the letter of the law and the gospel of grace. Let me explain the difference. The gospel of law is a gospel of performance, as in getting value from performance itself. One type of this gospel charges us with responsibility of living a good life and performing to get our value. There are as many types of this gospel showing up as rules or laws people base their lives on. Some people live their life performing to have value based on the rules and the laws of Christianity. Another person may believe the rules and laws of Muhammad are the right ones. And they live their life based on these. And yet another person has a set of business ethics and rules that they practice that they seek to perform to have value and be acceptable. These rules and laws under this gospel even extend to those practicing witchcraft or the New Age movement or various ideologies, as well as various types of Satanism.

All these sets of laws have a common thread. They give a person hope if they can achieve according to the standard of achievement, they have set for themselves. After all, Scripture does say *hope is the anchor of our soul.* (Heb. 6:19). Each one of these sets of laws is serving as an unstable anchor for all these and many more groups of people. Their hope is coming from their achievement of their standard or law. The problem with this gospel is it's based on man's determination of the right set of rules or laws that we determine through our filter evaluated by our carnal minds. In this Gospel Our value is based on how we perform based on these laws. There is a constant striving to achieve even if the rules and laws lived or believed are by very broken people practicing Satanism or evil practices or agendas. This striving is demonstrated in the Law of the Old Testament (in the Bible), all these sets of laws or rules create potential situations of falling short.

The common pattern is that no matter what law you are trying to achieve with this gospel, you will fall short because you will never be good enough. You will always be striving to achieve at a higher or different level to have value. There is never enough under this gospel. So to be justified you either condemn yourself or compare yourself to others to seek justification which often can bring condemnation instead.

I recognize that the Old Testament comes before the New Testament and serves as the type and shadow. The Old Testament is to lead us to the liberty of the New Testament and Jesus' shed blood on the cross making him our protector, not ourselves.

Under the first gospel, we are our own protector and provider, even though we may have some carnal and mental belief in another entity doing this. If we look at our actions, we are protecting ourselves.

We find in this gospel of self-protection lots of negative emotions that serve to help self-protect, such as anxiety or lots of dysfunctional types of fear and anger and depression and confusion, as well as lots of fast or racing thoughts in the mind. These are a result of self-protection. They are part of our self-protection system.

Scripture infers to us in Galatians that one of the reasons God gave us the law to show us that we can't keep the law and that we have a better Promise in Jesus Christ. One reason God gave us the law was that not able to keep the Law we would turn to him and he would be our protector, not ourselves.

> *But the Scripture has confined all under sin, that the promise by faith in Jesus Christ might be given to those who believe. But before faith came, we were kept under guard by the law, kept for the faith which would afterward be revealed." Galatians 3:22-23*

The second gospel is the gospel of liberty and freedom. This gospel lies on the foundation that Jesus, by his love and his sacrifice and his shed blood on the cross, has paid the full price for our past, present, and future sins, mistakes. He made us whole, pure, and complete through faith and trust in what he did is actually true.

In this gospel, there is no performance necessary to get

value. He did all the performance for us. The gospel says that everything is paid for by Jesus, not myself or others. I can't pay for these sins or mistakes, and I don't have to because he already did. This second gospel of grace says that my value was fully established from the beginning of time and he proved this by his full payment on the cross that no one could accuse me. That I can't have less value, it's impossible. No matter what I do or what is done to me, my value is full and complete in Jesus and can't change. This is the love he has for me. So as I know the love he has for me, I know my identity (my true self) which is who I am.

> *"And we have known and believed the love that God has for us. God is love, and he who abides in love abides in God, and God in him." 1 John 4:16*

When I know who I am, I can't sin because sin is not who I am. Sin is not who I am. It is not included with my true identity. I stop sinning not by trying harder not to sin but by knowing who I am by knowing God's love for me. This revelation of God's love not only releases my true identity but escorts me in the plans and the calls God has created me for. I do not need to make these plans happen. They are written on my DNA. They are written, Scripture says. I automatically do who I am when I trust him and know his love.

I believe no person can get in the way of the call of God on my life except for my own heart. Nothing can get in the way. Except for my own heart. But when I fully trust God, nothing can stop God's call in my life. No one can stop God and his plans for me. No one can trump God.

Trust or faith opens the doors for his plans and his promises to go forth. This Gospel is the true gospel, the Gospel of the Kingdom.

On a side note, when people say they don't believe in Jesus and his shed blood on the cross, most of the time they will not discuss it. When we verbally try to convince them, we are trying to convince their carnal mind, which we will not be able to convince. Arguing or debating is futility because often we are debating out of our carnal mind and our flesh. The carnal mind cannot evangelize the carnal mind. It is only by the spirit led by God's Spirit, the Holy Spirit, the word goes forth to move beyond their carnal mind into their spirit or their heart.

I believe there is a part of everyone's spirit that has some knowledge or connection to God even before we invite him in. There is a knowing that gets drawn out by their unbelieving flesh. After all, we are all created in his image by him.

CHAPTER 23

Moving Faith to a Community of Faith

I believe that God has a perfectly ordered plan that involves the beginning from the end. Since there is no time dimension in heaven, God sees it all at once with his heart focused on the truth, the perfectly ordered truth. His faith partnered with ours is now in a creation process to bring forth the truth, the perfectly ordered plan.

His plan not only includes physical creation, but it includes the creation of our trust and faith in him, along with bringing all creation to its truth and , its perfectly created fullness. God's creation in us and all creation is being birthed as we speak. Conception to birth in this process is a lot longer than nine months. But then again, there is no time dimension in the spirit, in God, in the Kingdom. God is not ruled by any dimensions.

"But, beloved, do not forget this one thing, that with the Lord one day [is] as a thousand years, and a thousand years as one day." 2 Pe 3:8 NKJV

"For the earnest expectation of the creation eagerly waits for the revealing of the sons of God." Rom 8:19 NKJV

One of the things we see in order is unity. As sons, we walk in perfect order, perfect harmony, according to God's perfect plan, without spot or wrinkle.

"...that He might present her to Himself a glorious church, not having spot or wrinkle or any such thing, but that she should be holy and without blemish." Eph 5:27 NKJV

As God brings unity and order in our hearts, we will be able to walk in that perfect unity with each other. We will walk and live by his plan and our value will not be anchored to performance.

"...the works were finished from the foundation of the world." Heb 4:3 NKJV

The results are up to God. He has already completed them in the Spirit realm.

As we walk in the spirit continuously, we will act according to who we are and it will not be in conflict with my brother or sister in Christ, as they walk in God's perfect order. We will trust God in all things and there will be no need to self-protect. I will know who I am and you will know who you are and there will be no conflict. We will rejoice in what each other carries and who they are and rejoice in each other's revelations. Our thankfulness will be constantly overflowing as we speak life and truth into one another, to propel each other in Christ to our call and our destiny.

As we step towards unity in the church, it looks a bit like stepping towards unity in our heart. There have been lots of focus on self-protection or self-will. Often we do not know when we are trusting God or trusting ourselves. We have lots of rules that we call wisdom, but individually do not know how to connect with God and each other intimately. We like to keep score to make sure others are treating us equally or what we would call fairly. We look to others to act in certain ways to help us feel wanted or valued. And if they don't, we're offended or hurt. We look to systems of communication to express our hearts and fix each other. We are guarded in what we say or how we express our visions and spirit-led feelings because we fear being rejected or cast out of the circle. We try to keep all the rules so we can anchor our values in our holiness or performance.

God's plan is to heal our hearts to walk in the spirit constantly. This not only will unify our hearts, but it will unify us as the body, as his body. We will be led by his Spirit of love separate from any agenda or need to perform to get love. As God orders our steps, we will walk in his perfect heartbeat to the perfect cadence, fully releasing his unconditional love. God has a plan and assignment for each one of us and together the Kingdom goes forth as we walk in his community of love. We are not dependent on those in the community to fulfill our needs; We are fully dependent on God for all our needs; even if they are being provided by those in the community, ultimately they are being provided for by God. Out of this deep and intimate connection with God, we love each other unconditionally. This includes outwardly releasing unconditional love to each other. It will be very common to see God do creative miracles all around us. In addition to the physical healings including new hearts, lungs and body parts for those we pray for, we will see diamonds from heaven and even physical buildings released from heaven, supernaturally, as we nurture each other with God's love released through us.

I know some of this may seem crazy, but for the God who created the universe, all things are possible. I will talk more about this in the next chapter on dimensions.

Unity of faith brings forth these creative miracles. We were created in God's image and as God has the capacity to create, he imparted this same capacity inside each one of us. As we trust what he says is true, we know Scripture says in John,

> *"Most assuredly, I say to you, he who believes in Me, the works that I do he will do also; and greater works than these he will do, because I go to My Father." John 14:12 NKJV*

> *"I am the vine, you [are] the branches. He who abides in Me, and I in him, bears much fruit; for without Me you can do nothing." Jn 15:5 NKJV*

And he talks about us being totally grafted in.

> *"And if some of the branches were broken off, and you, being a wild olive tree, were grafted in among them, and with them became a partaker of the root and fatness of the olive tree..." Rom 11:17 NKJV*

> *"...He who says he abides in Him ought himself also to walk just as He walked." 1 Jn 2:6 NKJV*

> *"that they all may be one, as You, Father, [are] in Me, and I in You; that they also may be one in Us, that the world may believe*

that You sent Me." Jn 17:21 NKJV

We are so used to living as natural men out of our own understanding and our own carnal mind that walking in community and unity in the spirit is a new paradigm. It takes trust and focus on Jesus to walk in the spirit and be who we really are, spirit people with a body, led by God's Spirit, the Holy Spirit. This unity in the Spirit will give us trust and faith way beyond even a mustard seed. Together we will move mountains.

In the Bible, we see unbelievers unite to build this extraordinary tower to heaven, the Tower of Babel. We see a picture of unity with the wrong spirit and the incredible physical and spiritual results that it produced. We know this tower was built out of performance to get value, or out of the flesh and self-protection. This performance focused on "my will be done," fully by self-will. It was undergirded by self-protection and not trusting God but instead putting faith and trust in themselves and others as their protectors and providers. Out of this, this tower of enormous size and proportion was built.

If we look at the types of unity created by the enemy's kingdom, it is focused on serving man and money. That has created unimaginable things from physical structures to the Internet, to the tiniest of computers or computer chips to mechanical human body parts that function in our bodies. All this is combining our God-given ability to create and to unify human effort for common goals, often to produce money or to fulfill the need for value in the individual. The motivator or driver in much of this is the broken heart and the flesh. We see this also in activities, such as sports. We see how the need for value motivates, leads and creates intensity. Yet all creativity or creation comes out of

God's revelation. We cannot create something new to God. It all comes from him and through him, even if we are not submitted to him and are motivated by our flesh.

The difficulty is that the use of these created things gets perverted and twisted to not be part of God's will, but the will of the flesh.

> *"For by Him all things were created that are in heaven and that are on earth, visible and invisible, whether thrones or dominions or principalities or powers. All things were created through Him and for Him." Col 1:16 NKJV*

When flesh creates apart from God's plan or God's will, I believe disorder comes to our world. Those created things often, if not always, function out of purpose, out of order apart from God's design. This multiplies brokenness in our world.

It is going to be extraordinary when we, as believers, take over the creation process fully in the spirit, releasing not only the creation but God's vision and purpose for each design. That doesn't mean that there were not believers in any creation process of all those things created up to today. Believers have released the creation process at times. I believe that, as we take over the creation process, what's going to happen is amazing and extraordinary as the kingdom comes forth.

> *"For the earnest expectation of the creation eagerly waits for the revealing of the sons of God... because the creation itself also will be delivered from the bondage of corruption into the glorious liberty of the children of God. For we know that the whole creation groans and labors with birth pangs together until now." Rom 8:19,21-22 NKJV*

Our motivation will not be money or power, control or those things of the flesh, but out of our love connection with God we will release what God created in us, the revelation we carry in our DNA. No one can get in the way of this creative process except for our broken heart.

I believe there already has been lots of this creation process done in the Spirit, but a small percentage of all those things created so far was in unity to bring forth the Kingdom.

The times will change as we trust God and as our hearts step into the deep healing, to operate out of our own revelations God has created us to release.

Healing the Heart, the Individual, and the Nations

CHAPTER 24

Dimensions

I refer to dimensions as those things in the physical, natural world that govern us or rule over us that God created to serve us. Physical structures have dimensional aspects, such as length, depth, width, height that serve as barriers.

Another type of dimension would be money or exchange. Money often rules over people. Most people serve money and are performing to get money for payments, for rent or to buy goods, even to the point of creating a promise of debt that says if I don't pay, you can take the house, the car, the furniture back. This arrangement then enslaves the person to perform and serve this debt, this desire to keep the house, the car, with hope that the person will derive some type of value or safety from keeping the leveraged item is a type of modern day slavery. With this arrangement our trust is in our ability to perform and make the money to pay the debt rather than in our Protector and Provider, God.

Another type of dimension would be time. We are governed by time. We serve time. We feel if we are on time for an appointment, we will have more value than if we don't show up on time.

Often our motivation for being on time is to maintain or gain value as a person. Because of our motivation to serve time, we will call time a dimension also. Dimensions are realities in the natural world. We serve these dimensions as a way to function within the natural world. Our reality, or what is true and real, can be the natural world. What we can physically see is what is real. This view of the world is what Scripture refers to as the natural man. (1 Cor. 2:14) The natural man is governed by his own lust or flesh. It also tells us in Scripture that those things that are seen are temporal and those things that are unseen are eternal.

> *"...while we do not look at the things which are seen, but at the things which are not seen. For the things which are seen [are] temporary, but the things which are not seen [are] eternal." 2 Cor. 4:18 NKJV*

We are spirit people, with a body, and God created us to walk in the spirit, not the flesh or the natural man.

Our spirit, led by God's Spirit, is meant to lead our body. Our flesh or our carnal mind was not God's plan to lead our body.

As we begin to live our lives out of the spirit, we are no longer governed by the dimensions created by the natural world.

Money or time in the natural man (world) is in charge and leads, however, as we walk in the spirit it begins to follow and serve us.

I believe even dimensions like length, width, height, and depth begin to serve us when God is our Protector and not us protecting ourselves. I look to him for my provision, not myself, as I walk in the spirit and he orders my steps.

Money, or provision, follows or shows up as needed while I walk out the call of God in the Spirit in my life.

> *"Therefore do not worry, saying, 'What shall we eat?' or 'What shall we drink?' or 'What shall we wear?' "Mat 6:31 NKJV*

> *"For My yoke is easy and My burden is light." Mat 11:30 NKJV*

In the Spirit I am not under the rules and laws of the natural kingdom. I live according to trust and faith in the Lord and his word by the Spirit, the Holy Spirit.

Faith and trust are like muscles and when I first begin to exercise, these faith muscles are not fully developed. As stated earlier, I have to develop them by exercising or stretching them. How do I do this? I step through the fears that cause me to protect myself. I step through my flesh and grab tightly and fully dependent on Jesus. As the feelings of flesh show up, I hold on and cry out to my Protector, Jesus, and eventually the flesh will die and my confidence and trust will grow. I will no longer protect myself but only look to Jesus to be my Protector in more and more areas, including money.

I'm not talking about staying in bed and isolating myself. I'm talking about an active process of crucifying the flesh, stepping through and choosing to actively step through and do those things in your body that fear and even your understanding does not track with.

For example, you have thoughts of moving to South Carolina to start a church, but you have no money or resources. We do not always know God's timing so we begin to step towards the move as we seek from God what faith steps to take. Eventually, by small steps and prayer, you end up in South Carolina running a church. This does not mean God can't do larger steps. He often will move you as your faith will allow and it's okay whatever the pace. If you need to take larger steps, he will convict your heart to take larger steps along with opening doors for deeper relationship at times. We make the choice and decisions on how big of steps to trust God for.

No matter the size of the steps, his love for you is exactly the same. In my life, I have seen God get me to a level of faith in an area of my life and then stretch me to the next level of trust or faith in that area.

To use money as an example, I believe God wants to release trillions of dollars to the church. The wealth of the wicked will be turned over to the righteous. (Prov.13:22) I have seen incredible financial things in my life by the hand of God that are tiny compared to what he wants to do and is going to do. Because of this, the financial stretches can reappear for a season to develop more trust at a bigger level as more and more flesh (self-protection) dies to make room for bigger provisions and release.

I talked earlier about the house God had released on the promised land, which was incredible, but to complete all the buildings and the architecture, the architect estimates could be $25 to $30 million. God is preparing for this type of faith.

Less than six years ago, the One Whole Heart Ministry and part of our ministry, Valor Christian Academy, received a large school building along with $65,000 in cash and approximately 15,000 valuable collectibles (worth about $200,000 to $250,000) from someone who didn't know anyone or anything about One Whole Heart Ministry. The estimated value of the gift is approximately $500,000 to $600,000 or more, counting the building, the cash, and the collectibles. This was incredible and supernatural.

I could go on about many other gifts or supernatural acts by God and I'm sure you yourself have several testimonies. The truth is, we can't anchor our faith and our value in the past testimonies or we will get stuck at that place. The testimonies are good to propel others' faith, but we must move on and realize God wants to keep multiplying this trust so we can release more and continuously release his provision to the church, his bride. This is necessary for the Kingdom to come forth.

Keep your eyes on what God does in the upcoming days and years. I believe you are going to see even more of the very powerful and wealthy (in our natural world) coming to faith in a big way in the near future. I believe God is about to move in these false kingdoms in a very big way and take dominion. I do not believe this will happens by God moving on the basis of it's time, I believe God sees the beginning from the end. Our hearts are beginning to trust him more and more and as our faith increases, this opens doors for God to release his Kingdom even in the power structures of society. As we trust him, money follows and serves us as his Kingdom comes forth.

Time is similar to money as a dimension. When we let go

of time and getting our value out of time and trust God for the fullness of our value, time also begins to serve us. This does not mean we do not have a structure or a schedule, but it means that our schedule is about and through him, God. As we walk fully in God's call or God's will for our life, with the full flexibility to change, he molds our environment around us, even our schedule, as he manages time. He places it in perfect sync and harmony.

I get a cancellation in one appointment, so someone else can receive ministry. Someone gets a flat tire on the way to an appointment and can't make it, so I can spend time with a staff person who needs encouragement and love. I notice the more I let go of time being in charge, the more peace and rest dwells and relationship can grow as God rearranges my schedule.

I first decided to trust in God instead of time about 15 years ago. I decided not to use an alarm clock but to trust God to wake me up each day. When I would have a 6 a.m. flight and have to be at the airport at four o'clock, I would pray and humbly ask the Holy Spirit to wake me up for my flight. God would always wake me up. The time was not exactly the time I asked, but when I needed to get up. Instead of waking up at three, it might be 2:45 or 3:15, but it would always be the right time.

A third group of dimensions we are going to talk about in this chapter is length, depth, width and height. I believe in the Spirit we are not ruled by matter or any of these dimensions. We are seated at the right hand of God in heavenly places. I will let you know right now, as of the date of the writing of this book, I have not in my visible physical body walked through a physical wall nor have I felt the Lord leading me to focus on that area of breakthrough.

I will say this, that God created even matter to serve us and not for us to serve it.

There are many times while driving I can't remember how I got to where I'm at. I believe often I have been in the Spirit, not only driving but doing other things. I remember one specific example driving when my flesh arose. I drove across Iowa to Illinois to buy a large 24-foot trailer with a four-ton tractor. As I began to drive, I felt like the weight and the activity of the tractor on the trailer was out of control. I gripped the steering wheel tight with a degree of fear. I remember knowing fear is not who I am and, looking to the Lord, I began to pray and worship. I arrived at home four hours later with no recall of the trip. I had disappeared into Jesus and into the Spirit.

Although I have had many experiences like this and I'm sure you have also, I personally am limited in my experiences breaking through this dimension. This does not make the reality of this and many other dimensions that are submissive to us less real, but only verifies that we are called to break through all the dimensions together. Each believer has a different call and together we can bring each other into our breakthroughs.

In conclusion, as we begin to walk in who we are, we will break through the dimensions and serve God as we are constantly in his Spirit, walking in the Holy Spirit, and not being governed by the natural laws. Not only this, but we will live in the Spirit of Jesus, which is love, and in this walk his Kingdom will come forth. We have to realize that many of the things others have experienced or walked in are real and God is the author of them experiences like traveling in the Spirit (the Holy Spirit) or commanding the physical realm to obey certain actions or commands. We have attributed a lot of this to the New Age or witchcraft or the occult. The problem is that what they are doing is going into the spirit realm not connected through our Lord Jesus Christ our Savior. They are entering the sheepgate through another door.

> *"Most assuredly, I say to you, he who does not enter the sheepfold by the door, but climbs up some other way, the same is a thief and a robber. But he who enters by the door is the shepherd of the sheep. To him the doorkeeper opens, and the sheep hear his voice; and he calls his own sheep by name and leads them out. And when he brings out his own sheep, he goes before them; and the sheep follow him, for they know his voice. Yet they will by no means follow a stranger, but will flee from him, for they do not know the voice of strangers." Jn 10:1-5 NKJV*

They are entering the sheepgate through another spirit, other than Jesus. That's divination and a very sad and potentially painful situation for them. They are acting on true realities through the wrong spirit. There is only one door: Jesus. By Christian believers being afraid of the things that are real in the spirit realm, we are denying ourselves those things created by God for the body of Christ and forcing ourselves to walk in the carnal-minded, flesh-driven person. This is not God's Kingdom. It is Satan's attempt at a kingdom. We are created to walk in the Spirit and be who we really are. By walking in the flesh we are walking as the natural man instead of the Spirit man. It is the "wrong kingdom." We have to be open to who we are, the way we were created, and realize that Satan is a thief and steals the things of God and perverts them. He has no original creation. We cannot let him steal who we are, "the real us." We need to start taking back what belongs to us, including walking in the Holy Spirit. By walking in the Spirit, we can't sin. That's our true identity. Walking in the Spirit brings unity, love, and empowerment, to be who we are created to be, God's true design and order. Out of all of this, hearts are healed, relationships healed, and the Kingdom of God comes forth.

CHAPTER 25

Healing the Broken Places

As I wrote about earlier, self-protection shuts down relationship. As we self-protect, we shut down communication and
become self-focused. That is the flesh. Scripture tells us the
tongue (flesh) is wicked beyond all things. No man tames the
tongue (flesh) (Jer 17:9, Jas 3:8). It also tells us:

> *"A good man out of the good treasure of his heart brings forth good;*
> *and an evil man out of the evil treasure of his heart brings forth*
> *evil. For out of the abundance of the heart his mouth speaks. "*
> *Luke 6:45*

The other direction is to love unto God being our Protector in all things. This is being God-focused, "thy will be done."
Out of this connection with God, we constantly look to him,
connecting to him and his heart in total dependency and love.

Unconditional love is the fruit of trusting God and intimately connecting with him as our one and only Protector. With this love (connection to God), we can love those around us unconditionally. God's love in us produces thankfulness and compassion. Instead of comparing ourselves to others and looking at others' faults to try to create value in ourselves, we see those around us with God's compassion. We see them as God sees them, as who they really are and not the places where they're falling short.

We also need to understand the presence of God changes the atmosphere and even those around us react differently. Knowing this, it is also important to understand that broken relationships do not heal through trying to fix each other out of the carnal mind or out of our own understanding. Love covers a multitude of sins. Unconditional love is what brings healing, which is demonstrated by physical touch and kind, unconditional words of love. Correcting words are normally self-protection and fuel broken relationships.

I believe in relationship, physically holding each other in intimate relationship, is needed to open hearts, especially a marriage relationship. Words often create conflict at the place of brokenness. Embracing and physical safe touch can break down barriers, not only in a marriage relationship but in community relationships. Eventually, using this revelation that God is our Protector and not using anger, hiding, or disconnecting, would help allow the relationship becomes safer for those involved.

As we express our unconditional love in this way it will be time to express internal feelings to one another when the softening of the heart of the other person has opened the door of communication and they are not going to self-protect. We have connected the hearts and brought safety into the relationship by always walking in the Spirit, listening and going to God for revelation and vision on how to love on a safer level and by releasing unconditional Love not tied to expectations or not trying to change each other.

It's God's job to create change in our heart. We can't do that. By choosing to love this way, both people are empowering each other by giving each other a voice.

The root of most broken relationships is internal and external anger. It is anger towards the other person or even those people we grew up with that took away our voices. We empower and love each other when we stop self-protecting and give each other their voice back. We help them to understand that they are heard and have a voice and a choice, not only before God, because they've never lost their voice before God, but before us in our relationship.

If we look at this approach of broken relationships, we can treat broken relationships between churches, people, groups, countries, classes or genders the same way. Love covers a multitude of sins and God is our Protector in all types of relationship.